A TEACHER'S GUIDE TO

STICK UP FOR YOURSELF!

EVERY KID'S GUIDE TO PERSONAL POWER

AND POSITIVE SELF-ESTEEM

A 10-PART COURSE IN SELF-ESTEEM AND ASSERTIVENESS FOR KIDS

Gershen Kaufman, Ph.D., Lev Raphael, Ph.D.,
and Pamela Espeland

free spirit
PUBLISHING®

Helping kids
help themselves™
since 1983

At the time of this book's publication, all facts and figures cited are the most current available; all telephone numbers, addresses, and Web site URLs are accurate and active; all publications, organizations, Web sites, and other resources exist as described in this book; and all have been verified as of August 2003. The authors and Free Spirit Publishing make no warranty or guarantee concerning the information and materials given out by organizations or content found at Web sites, and we are not responsible for any changes that occur after this book's publication. If you find an error or believe that a resource listed here is not as described, please contact Free Spirit Publishing. Parents, teachers, and other adults: We strongly urge you to monitor children's use of the Internet.

Cover design by Percolator
Book design and typesetting by Dao Nguyen

10 9 8 7 6 5
Printed in the United States of America

Free Spirit Publishing Inc.
217 Fifth Avenue North, Suite 200
Minneapolis, MN 55401-1299
(612) 338-2068
help4kids@freespirit.com
www.freespirit.com

CONTENTS

LIST OF REPRODUCIBLE PAGES

INTRODUCTION

WHAT IS SELF—ESTEEM AND WHY SHOULD WE TEACH IT?. . . . .

Positive self-esteem is the single most important psychological skill we can develop in order to thrive in society. Having self-esteem means being proud of ourselves and experiencing that pride from within. Without self-esteem, kids doubt themselves, cave in to peer pressure, feel worthless or inferior, and may turn to drugs or alcohol as a crutch. With self-esteem, kids feel secure inside themselves, are more willing to take positive risks, are more likely to take responsibility for their actions, can cope with life's changes and challenges, and are resilient in the face of rejection, disappointment, failure, and defeat.

Self-esteem is *not* conceit, it's *not* arrogance, and it's *not* superiority. Unfortunately, it's often confused with all three (and also with narcissism, egotism, and disrespect), which has contributed to a "self-esteem backlash." You've probably seen the articles and heard the assertions that too much self-esteem is bad for kids. Nothing could be further from the truth. Indiscriminate praise, flattery, social promotion, and falsely inflated self-worth are bad for kids, but those aren't what self-esteem is about. Self-esteem is based on facts and truths, achievements and competencies. The more self-esteem kids have, and the stronger it is, the better equipped they are to make their way in the world.

Conceit, arrogance, and superiority aren't the result of genuine pride. They are the result of *contempt* for others. Pride grows out of enjoying ourselves, our accomplishments, our skills and abilities. It's not about diminishing anyone else.

Contempt often masquerades as pride, but it's a false pride. When we're contemptuous of others, we perceive them as being beneath us. Secretly, however, we feel *inferior* to others. Contempt allows us to rise above those feelings of inferiority temporarily, but in order to keep feeling this way, we must continually find someone else to feel superior to—someone else we can put down in order to stay on top.

We believe that contempt is a root cause of two great problems facing our schools (and our world) today: bullying and violence. Bullies who taunt, tease, and harass others aren't kids with positive self-esteem and genuine pride in themselves. They are kids who lack social skills and empathy and may have other serious problems, including parents or older siblings who bully them, deep-seated anger, jealousy of other people's success, and loneliness. In order to bully others, you must believe that their feelings, wants, and needs don't matter. You must feel contempt for them.

When contempt combines with feelings of powerlessness and shame, this may (and often does) escalate into violence. We've seen this in the school shootings that have shocked us so profoundly in recent years. The children and teens who wounded and killed their classmates and teachers weren't kids with positive self-esteem and genuine pride in themselves. Some were bullied, tormented, and humiliated by their peers; some were rejected, excluded, and ignored. For reasons we may never fully understand, these kids developed absolute contempt for others, coupled with a desire for vengeance. It wasn't just that other people's feelings, wants, and needs didn't matter. Their *lives* didn't matter.

Self-esteem isn't the culprit here. Rather, the *lack* of positive self-esteem may lead some kids to take inappropriate, hurtful, even desperate actions. When we help kids build self-esteem, we're not teaching them to diminish others, and we're certainly not teaching them to be contemptuous. We're teaching them to take pride in themselves, feel good about themselves when they do the right thing (and own responsibility when they don't), celebrate their achievements (both tangible and intangible), know what they stand for (and what they won't stand for), and strive to be their best inside and out. When kids have a solid grasp of their feelings and needs, when they trust their emotions and perceptions, when they have a realistic sense of their capabilities, and when they have personal power—they feel secure and confident inside themselves—there's no need to put other people down.

Self-esteem isn't something we're born with. It's something we learn, which means it can be taught. We believe that all children should be taught the skills of personal power and positive self-esteem at home and in the classroom, right along with reading, writing, and arithmetic. All of these "basics" work hand-in-hand.

ABOUT THIS BOOK . . . .

A Teacher's Guide to Stick Up for Yourself! helps children and youth in grades 3–7 build self-esteem, become more self-aware, and develop and practice assertiveness skills. It was designed for the classroom, but it can also be used in other group settings, including counseling groups, after-school programs, youth groups, clubs, and community programs.

It is intended to be used with the student book, *Stick Up for Yourself! Every Kid's Guide to Personal Power and Positive Self-Esteem.* Students are asked to read portions of that book before and/or during each session, so you'll want to have several copies on hand if at all possible. Ideally, each student will have his or her own copy.

The student book is based on a program originally developed for adults. Called "Affect and Self-Esteem," it is currently offered as an undergraduate course in the Psychology Department at Michigan State University. For *Stick Up for Yourself!*, we adapted the course materials for ages 8–12. By reading the book and doing the "Get Personal" writing exercises, children can learn essential self-esteem concepts on their own. That learning becomes especially powerful in a classroom or group setting, where children benefit from the guidance of a caring adult leader and the opportunity to explore the concepts more fully in activities and discussions.

A Teacher's Guide includes clear and complete instructions for ten consecutive sessions. Each session is presented in a logically organized, step-by-step way. The sessions are scripted so you can literally read many parts aloud, if you like. Our goal was to create a guide that would be welcoming and easy to use for any classroom teacher or adult group leader, beginning or experienced.

A Teacher's Guide also includes suggestions for additional curriculum-related activities and a list of resources.

ABOUT THE SESSIONS............................

The sessions are:

1: What Does It Mean to Stick Up for Yourself?
2: You Are Responsible for Your Behavior and Feelings
3: Making Choices
4: Naming Your Feelings
5: Claiming Your Feelings
6: Naming and Claiming Your Dreams
7: Naming and Claiming Your Needs
8: Getting and Using Power
9: Building Self-Esteem
10: Sticking Up for Yourself from Now On

Each session includes the following parts:

- **Overview:** Introduces and briefly describes the session topic(s).
- **Learner Outcomes:** States the purpose of the session and what your students should be able to do after participating in the session.

- **Materials:** Lists all of the materials (handouts, writing materials, etc.) you and your students will need for the session.

- **Agenda:** Gives you an at-a-glance plan for the entire session.

- **Activities:** Guides you step-by-step through the session, from introduction through closing. Each activity relates to one or more of the learner outcomes.

GENERAL GUIDELINES

1. Familiarize yourself with the entire course before you lead the first session. Read this introduction and "Getting Ready" (pages 8–13) first, then read through all ten sessions and "Additional Activities Across the Curriculum" (pages 116–118). Depending on how much time you have before the course begins, you may want to consult one or more of the resources listed on pages 119–120.

2. Give yourself time to prepare for each session. Make sure you have all the materials you need, including enough copies of any handout(s) used in the session.

3. Make use of the generous margins in this guide. They're here for a reason: to give you plenty of space to jot down notes, observations, personal experiences, additional questions, ideas, reactions, and anything else that comes to mind. We hope you'll customize this guide and make it your own.

4. Keep parents informed about what you're doing in the course. Invite their questions before, during, and after. See "Informing and Involving Parents and Caregivers" (pages 8–9).

5. Remember that as a caring, concerned adult, you're in a perfect position to help students build personal power and positive self-esteem. Treat them with respect. Encourage them to do their best—without expecting perfection. Allow them to make mistakes and take positive risks. Give them opportunities to make choices and decisions. Invite them to share their feelings, needs, and future dreams. Be someone they trust and can talk to about things that matter to them.

YOUR ROLE AS TEACHER

In this course, the teaching role may be somewhat different than what you're used to. You'll structure the activities and organize the physical setting, just as you do in other teaching situations. But the students, in a sense, will determine the content. Their life experiences will form the basis for discussion.

For this reason, you may feel somewhat apprehensive about your ability to respond and to teach. You may not feel the same self-assurance you have in other teaching situations. Two things may help you:

1. being willing to serve as a model for your students, and

2. being familiar with the tools presented in the course.

We have found that teachers who are willing to serve as models by sharing their own experiences and feelings are more effective as facilitators. Plus they come away from the course feeling that something significant has happened for everyone, including themselves.

Modeling means letting students see that you, too, have situations in your life that require you to sort through your feelings, figure out which needs are important to meet at the time, and so on. It doesn't necessarily mean sharing in every activity. But whenever you see an opportunity to help students understand by sharing a personal experience or feeling, do it.

The tools presented in the course include the Happiness List (pages 30–32), the I-Did-It List (pages 70–72), and the methods for talking things over with yourself (pages 58–59, 69–70, and 81–82). Practice using the tools yourself so you're able to model them for students. If you start writing your own Happiness List and I-Did-It List each day, you'll have examples to share with students when those tools are introduced.

YOUR ROLE AS DISCUSSION LEADER

1. As teacher, you provide the structure. Be clear about the purpose of each session, and let the students know that it's your role to keep the session moving along.

2. It's important to try to give everyone who wants to share an opportunity to do so. But sometimes you'll need to move on before a student has said everything he or she wants to. When this happens, say "I'll come back to you if there's time."

3. Sometimes students will want to share their thoughts and feelings; sometimes they won't. Let them know it's okay to say "I pass." At the same time, encourage students to share whenever they feel comfortable doing so, because sharing allows the group to offer feedback and support. Point out that we also learn a lot by listening.

4. Model support and encouragement when students are talking. Don't judge what they say. Sometimes you may want to point out choices they have, but never tell them which choice they *should* make or what they *should* think. Notice even small ways students are learning and growing, and comment favorably on them.

5. Try not to talk too much; this group is for the students, and you want them to participate. When you have something to say, keep it short and to the point, then reinvolve the students in the discussion.

6. Ask open-ended questions, not those that can be answered with a yes or no. For example, you might ask "How would you feel if…?" rather than "Would you be upset if…?"

7. If you want to bring up a personal experience without identifying it as yours, you can begin by saying "I have a friend who…."

8. If someone monopolizes the discussion, gently direct attention away from him or her. You might say "Thank you for sharing. Now let's hear what other group members are thinking."

9. Find ways to involve everyone. If you have a student who isn't ready to participate in discussions, find another role for him or her. Let the student hand out papers or arrange chairs, or ask the student to help you remember to do something.

10. It helps to see life—yours and your students'—as a journey. What you see and hear and learn along the way is amazing. If you can communicate that to students, it may help them accept change as a natural, desirable process.

CHILD PROTECTION LAWS

Confidentiality is important to the success of this course, but there are certain things you may hear or observe that you *must* report for the protection of the child and any others involved.

Before beginning the course, be absolutely clear that you know what you're legally required to report and what the guidelines for reporting are. These reporting requirements usually fall under the category of child protection legislation.

Most school districts and youth organizations have developed guidelines to conform to child protection laws. Learn what those guidelines are and who you should report to if the need arises.

ABOUT THE EVALUATIONS

It's likely that you'll teach this course more than once, and you'll want to improve each time you teach it. Evaluations provide valuable feedback you can use to strengthen the course and your teaching.

This book includes two formal evaluations: one for students and one for parents (see pages 114 and 115). You might use information from completed evaluations to follow up after the course and plan future courses.

Students also have the opportunity to do a self-evaluation. During the first session, they are asked to write about particular situations for which they would like to learn how to stick up for themselves. During the final session, they are asked to read what they wrote during the first session and decide for themselves if they reached their goal(s). This helps students integrate their experience and realize what they have accomplished in the course.

GETTING SUPPORT FOR YOURSELF

In a course such as this, where feelings are expressed openly, you can't always anticipate what a session will be like or what needs may be revealed. Things may happen that indicate the need for follow-up, but you might not be sure how to proceed. For example, you may suspect that a child is showing signs of depression, but you're not sure if your hunch is accurate. Or you may notice that one student seems to have a great deal of anxiety. Or you may wonder, based on what a student shares in the group, whether there's a need for counseling or further discussion. Or you may not know what to do about a student who tends to be disruptive, but only in small-group settings. Or you may feel overwhelmed or drained by a particularly emotional session.

Think of someone you can talk to—a school counselor, the school psychologist, another teacher who has led similar classes, or another colleague you trust and respect. Ask if he or she is available to help you debrief after sessions when you feel the need. You can talk about what went on, but you'll want to respect the group's confidentiality, just as you expect the students to do.

For more information about some of the principles presented in this course, you may want to read *Dynamics of Power: Fighting Shame and Building Self-Esteem* by Gershen Kaufman and Lev Raphael. See page 120.

GETTING READY

SCHEDULING THE SESSIONS . . . .

If possible, schedule the sessions for a time when you can keep outside interruptions to a minimum. For example, try to avoid holding the sessions during a period of the day when class members are regularly called out of the room for various reasons. It's frustrating to get students involved and interested only to be distracted. Especially when feelings are being shared, it's disruptive to have people coming in and out who aren't part of the group and aren't aware of the discussion guidelines.

TIME REQUIREMENTS . . . .

Each session should take about 30–45 minutes from start to finish. The actual time required will depend on the amount of discussion that takes place during the activities.

As you teach the course for the first time, you may want to keep track of how long each session takes so you have this information when you teach the course again.

INFORMING AND INVOLVING PARENTS AND CAREGIVERS . . . .

At least one week before the course begins, send home a letter to parents and caregivers describing the course and telling them when it will start. A sample letter is found on page 12. You may copy and send this letter or use it as a starting point for your own letter. Depending on your situation, you may want to ask parents/caregivers for their support, and you may need to get their written permission for children to take the course.

Encourage parents/caregivers to read the student book, *Stick Up for Yourself! Every Kid's Guide to Personal Power and Positive Self-Esteem*. Tell students that their parents/caregivers may ask to borrow the book, and suggest that they take it home with them. If parents/caregivers want to look at the book before the course begins, arrange for them to see a copy.

Invite parents/caregivers to call you with any questions they have before, during, or after the course. Give them a phone number where they can reach you, and let them know the best times to call.

If you're teaching a group that is new to you, you may want to ask parents/caregivers if there's anything they would like you to know about their children before the class begins.

It's a good idea to stay in touch with parents/caregivers during the course. Consider sending home brief notes about how the course is progressing, or copying parents on handouts you use with the students. At the end of the course, invite feedback and comments from parents/caregivers by sending them an evaluation form (page 115).

PREPARING THE ROOM

The physical setting is important to the success of the course. Try to organize the room so you can, if possible, sit in a circle for group discussions. Allow space between small groups, but keep it organized so you're able to monitor what's going on in all of the groups.

Think about how you might signal the beginning of the session. Turning the lights off and on is one way to get your students' attention. You might play a few moments of relaxing music to let them know it's time to begin. Whatever you choose, you want it to be a pleasant way to shift gears.

GROUP DISCUSSION GUIDELINES

You may already have guidelines in place for class or group discussions. If so, make sure that everyone understands them and agrees with them. For the purposes of this course, your guidelines should include the following:

1. What is said in the group stays in the group.*

2. We are polite and respectful to each other. We don't use put-downs. We want everyone in the group to feel valued and accepted.

3. We listen to each other. When someone is talking, we look at the person and pay attention. We don't think about what we're going to say when it's our turn.

---

* See "Child Protection Laws," page 6.

4. Everyone is welcome to share their thoughts and feelings. But no one *has to share*. It's okay to say "I pass" if you don't want to share.

5. There are no right or wrong answers.

RELATING ACTIVITIES TO YOUR GROUP ....

Good teachers are flexible and responsive, and the success of this course doesn't depend on teaching it to the letter. As you plan for each session, think about ways you might adapt the activities to your students' needs and relate the examples to their interests. You may decide to modify an activity or example, to ask additional questions or substitute new questions. You may choose to replace or skip some of the activities. Keep the learner outcomes in mind when making changes to the sessions; let them guide your planning.

Many of the activities revolve around students' discussion of their own life experiences. This has a side benefit of automatically relating the course to the community in which they live. If students can't relate to an activity, they won't be able to use it as a springboard, and the discussion may fall flat. Often a minor change is all that's needed to help them see the connection between the activity and their lives. Take time to read through all the activities for a session before you conduct the session. If you feel that a particular activity isn't relevant to your students and their community, change it so it is.

USING THE "GET PERSONAL" ACTIVITIES ....

The student book includes several writing activities titled "Get Personal." (For examples, see *Stick Up for Yourself!* pages 26, 41, 46, 50, etc.) You might use these as optional activities during the course, or assign them when assigning students' reading for each session. Either way, make it clear that students' "Get Personal" writing will remain personal and confidential. Emphasize that they never have to share it with anyone (including you) unless they choose to.

Encourage students to think of the "Get Personal" activities as things they can do now and may want to do again, after the course is finished. Point out that their ideas and feelings will be changing along the way, and they may find they have new things to write about.

At a minimum, ask students to read the tips at the bottom of page 6 in *Stick Up for Yourself!* These briefly explain why the "Get Personal" activities are important and how to make the most of them.

BEFORE THE FIRST SESSION ....

A week before the course begins:

1. Tell students that next week you'll be starting a new course that will help them build self-esteem and be more assertive. Keep this announcement brief; explain that students will learn more once the course begins. Say that they'll need to bring a notebook to the first session, but that's all the preparing they'll have to do.

2. Send home a letter to parents and caregivers announcing the course. See "Informing and Involving Parents and Caregivers" (pages 8–9). You may want to attach a copy of "Session Topics and Reading Assignments" (page 13).

A day or two before the course begins:

1. Remind students that the course will start on (date), and ask them to be sure to bring a notebook to the first session.

2. Make copies of the "Session Topics and Reading Assignments" handout (page 13) and give one to each student (or wait until the first session to do this). You may want to add dates or other information about location and times. If students will be sharing copies of *Stick Up for Yourself! Every Kid's Guide to Personal Power and Positive Self-Esteem*, post a copy of the handout on the reading table.

Dear Parents/Caregivers,

I'm writing to tell you about an exciting new course called "Stick Up for Yourself!" that the children and I will be starting soon.

This ten-session course helps kids build self-esteem, become more self-aware, and develop and practice assertiveness skills. It teaches them to be responsible for their own behavior and feelings. Through readings, activities, and discussions, kids learn how to make good choices, get to know themselves better, handle strong feelings (like anger and jealousy), and form more positive relationships with the people in their lives (including you).

I want to make it very clear that this course does *not* teach kids to be conceited, arrogant, or disrespectful. That's not what self-esteem is about. Instead, it's about having the skills and strength to resist negative peer pressure, take positive risks, cope with life's changes and challenges, and feel proud of one's own accomplishments and abilities. We all need self-esteem to survive and thrive in today's world…and the earlier we learn it, the better.

You may want to read the book your child will be reading during the course. I encourage you to do so. It's called *Stick Up for Yourself! Every Kid's Guide to Personal Power and Self-Esteem.* Ask your child if you can borrow his or her copy. Or contact me and I'll arrange to get you a loaner copy right away.

This course can be a wonderful growing experience for your child. You may notice that he or she is "trying on" new behaviors and ways of relating to you or others in the family. Sometimes new behaviors are awkward; change takes time. You may see a new behavior one day and wonder where it went the next. When this happens, it might help to think about those times in our adult lives when we try to make changes. Changing is often slow for us, too.

Please feel free to call me with any questions you have before, during, or after the course.

Yours sincerely,

_____

Telephone: _____

Best times to reach me are: _____

The course begins on: _____

P.S. Students want their parents to *know about* the course, but they don't always want to *talk about* it while they're taking it. I suggest you let your child bring it up in discussions with you or your family. Please be patient!

SESSION TOPICS AND READING ASSIGNMENTS

All readings are from *Stick Up for Yourself! Every Kid's Guide to Personal Power and Positive Self-Esteem.*

Session	Reading
1. What Does It Mean to Stick Up for Yourself?	pages **1–4** (through "What You Need to Stick Up for Yourself")
2. You Are Responsible for Your Behavior and Feelings	pages **8–15** pages **86–90** (starting with "How to Live Happily Ever After")
3. Making Choices	pages **16–20**
4. Naming Your Feelings	pages **21–45** (through "Talk About Your Feelings")
5. Claiming Your Feelings	pages **57–71** (starting with "Claim Your Feelings, Future Dreams, and Needs")
6. Naming and Claiming Your Dreams	pages **45–48** (starting with "Name Your Future Dreams") pages **57–60** (starting with "Claim Your Feelings, Future Dreams, and Needs") pages **97–100** (starting with "Keep an I-Did-It List")
7. Naming and Claiming Your Needs	pages **49–60**
8. Getting and Using Power	pages **72–86** (up to "How to Live Happily Ever After")
9. Building Self-Esteem	pages **91–97** (up to "Keep an I-Did-It List") pages **101–110**
10. Sticking Up for Yourself from Now On	no reading assignment

THE SESSIONS

SESSION ONE
WHAT DOES IT MEAN TO STICK UP FOR YOURSELF?

OVERVIEW

Stick Up for Yourself!
Reading Assignment
pages 1–4 (through
"What You Need to
Stick Up for Yourself")

This session introduces the course. Students learn what "stick up for yourself" means. They discover that it doesn't mean getting back at someone else; being bossy, stuck-up, or rude; or saying and doing whatever you want, whenever you want. It means knowing who you are and what you stand for; being true to yourself; knowing how to speak up for yourself, and doing so when it's the right thing to do; and understanding that there's always someone on your side—*you*.

Students are introduced to the idea that the two things they need to stick up for themselves are personal power and positive self-esteem. Throughout the course, they will learn to develop these two important skills.

LEARNER OUTCOMES

The purpose of this session is to help students:

- prepare for the course
- become familiar with the phrase "stick up for yourself" as it is used in this course
- identify situations in which they feel they need to learn new ways to stick up for themselves

MATERIALS

- *Optional:* copies of the "Group Discussion Guidelines" handout (page 22) [activity 1]
- *Optional:* copies of the "Session Topics and Reading Assignments" handout (page 13) [activity 1]
- chalkboard or flip chart [activities 2, 4, 6]
- copies of the student book, *Stick Up for Yourself!* [activity 3]

- a blank piece of paper for each student [activity 5]
- student notebooks; have extras available for students who forget to bring their own [activity 6]

AGENDA ·

1. Orient students to the course.

2. Ask students to brainstorm what it means to stick up for yourself.

3. Give students time to read pages 1–4 in the student book (through "What You Need to Stick Up for Yourself").

4. Reexamine the list students made when brainstorming to see if their reading changed their ideas about what it means to stick up for yourself.

5. Lead the activity "Mix Up," in which situations and ways to stick up for yourself are randomly (and sometimes humorously) matched.

6. Ask students to identify and write down their goals for the course.

7. Close the session and assign the reading for Session 2.

ACTIVITIES ·

1. ORIENTATION

Say:

> **When you're finished with this course, you'll have a better understanding of what it means to stick up for yourself.**
>
> **You'll learn about things you can do and say—right now and in the future—to stick up for yourself.**
>
> **Each time we meet, you'll do some reading and write in your notebook. Be sure to have your notebook with you at every session.**
>
> **Before we start, let's make sure we all agree on some basic guidelines.**

Review your class discussion guidelines, or hand out copies of "Group Discussion Guidelines" and go over them with the students. *Tip:* During future sessions, you may want to post a copy of these guidelines where everyone can see it, to serve as a reminder.

Say:

> **You are encouraged to take part in all of the activities and discussions. Sometimes that will mean choosing to share your ideas and thoughts. Other times it may mean just being here and listening. Either response is okay.**
>
> **In this course, we will often spend time listening to each other. It is very important that we all show respect for each other.**

If you feel your students need specifics about what it means to be respectful, take a moment to go over those now. *Examples:* Pay attention; don't interrupt; don't sigh or make faces; don't use hurtful words; don't criticize or judge; treat other people as you want them to treat you.

Hand out copies of "Session Topics and Reading Assignments" if you didn't distribute these earlier.

2. WHAT DOES "STICK UP FOR YOURSELF" MEAN?

Ask:

> **What do you think it means to stick up for yourself?**

Write students' ideas on a chalkboard or flip chart, without commenting or asking for clarification.

3. READING

Ask students to read or review pages 1–4 in *Stick Up for Yourself!* (through "What You Need to Stick Up for Yourself"). Tell them to close their books when they're done so you'll be able to tell they're ready to go on.

4. WHAT DOES "STICK UP FOR YOURSELF" MEAN? (continued)

Go back to the list students brainstormed before reading. Say:

> **After reading, you may have changed your mind about what it means to stick up for yourself. Let's look at the list we made earlier.**
>
> **Now we know that sticking up for yourself doesn't mean getting back at someone else. Is there anything on our list that we might want to change? Anything that might suggest wanting revenge instead of sticking up for ourselves?**

Sticking up for yourself doesn't mean acting bossy, stuck-up, or rude. Is there anything on this list we might want to change?

Sticking up for yourself means knowing who you are and what you stand for, and being true to yourself. Are those on our list?

Can you give some examples of things you stand for? What does it mean to be true to yourself?

Speaking up for yourself is one way to stick up for yourself. Is that on our list?

Think about these words: "There's always someone on your side—*you*." What does this mean to you? Should we add this to our list?

5. MIX UP

Give each student a blank piece of paper.

Count off by threes (1, 2, 3, 1, 2, 3, and so on) until each member of the class has a number.

Ask the 1s to raise their hands. Say:

Think of a name of a popular actor or actress or cartoon character. Write the name on your paper.

Ask the 2s to raise their hands. Say:

Think of a situation you might get into at home, at school, or at a friend's house in which you might have to stick up for yourself. Write it on your paper.

Brainstorm with the 2s for a moment if they need help. Here are ideas to share:

- Your older brother borrowed your favorite CD or tape without asking.

- Your teacher lost your homework assignment and gave you a zero.

- Your mom forgot to pick you up after football practice.

- The bus driver threw you off the bus because he thought you were shoving and pushing.

Ask the 3s to raise their hands. Say:

Think of a way you would stick up for yourself. Write it on your paper.

Show the 3s the list the class made earlier if they need help.

Ask the students to get into groups of 3. Each group should have a 1, a 2, and a 3. Say:

Now we'll go around the room, giving each group a turn. You'll each read what is on your paper. Number 1 reads the name of the character. Number 2 tells us the situation the character is in. Number 3 tells us what the character will do. Just read what's on your paper, starting with Number 1. Do it quickly. Ready? Let's go.

End the activity by saying:

Sometimes what we do to stick up for ourselves works; sometimes it doesn't.

Sometimes we're hooked into ideas of how to stick up for ourselves and aren't aware of other ways. Sometimes we notice how other people stick up for themselves.

Sticking up for yourself isn't always something other people can see or hear.

6. GOAL SETTING

Write on the chalkboard or flip chart:

In this course, I want to learn new ways
to stick up for myself when...

Ask students to take out the notebooks they brought with them for the course. (Hand out extras to students who forgot theirs.) Say:

Copy this sentence starter into your notebook. Then take a few minutes to finish the sentence. At the end of the course, you'll look back at what you wrote to see if you learned what you hoped to learn.

7. CLOSING

Write on the chalkboard or flip chart:

> Personal power (knowing who you are)
> Positive self-esteem (liking yourself)

Summarize by saying:

> **In this session, we started learning what it means to stick up for yourself. These two things—personal power and positive self-esteem—will help you stick up for yourself, wherever you are, whatever situation you are in.**
>
> **In the next session, we'll begin talking about personal power.**
>
> **Before the next session, read pages 8 through 15 and 86 through 90 (starting with "How to Live Happily Ever After") in _Stick Up for Yourself!_**

If necessary, tell students where and when the next session will be.

GROUP DISCUSSION GUIDELINES

1. What is said in the group stays in the group.

2. We are polite and respectful to each other. We don't use put-downs. We want everyone in the group to feel valued and accepted.

3. We listen to each other. When someone is talking, we look at the person and pay attention. We don't think about what we're going to say when it's our turn.

4. Everyone is welcome to share their thoughts and feelings. But no one *has to share*. It's okay to say "I pass" if you don't want to share.

5. There are no right or wrong answers.

SESSION TWO

YOU ARE RESPONSIBLE FOR YOUR BEHAVIOR AND FEELINGS

OVERVIEW ....

Stick Up for Yourself!
Reading Assignment
pages 8–15 and 86–90
(starting with
"How to Live Happily
Ever After")

In this session, personal power is defined as "being secure and confident inside yourself." Personal power is presented as something that everyone can develop. Students learn that personal power has four parts: being responsible, making choices, getting to know yourself, and getting and using power in your relationships and your life.

This session is devoted to the first part: being responsible, specifically for your behavior and feelings. Students learn that even though other people may sometimes do or say things we respond to with a certain feeling or behavior, they didn't *make* us respond in that way. Similarly, even though other people respond to what we say or do in a certain way, we didn't *make* them do it. Each of us is responsible for our own behavior and feelings. At the same time, students learn that being responsible isn't the same as being perfect.

One of the principal tools used in the course, the Happiness List, is introduced as a powerful way to begin storing and collecting good feelings. This helps us develop personal power and positive self-esteem.

LEARNER OUTCOMES ....

The purpose of this session is to help students:

- identify that being responsible for their feelings and behavior is one way to develop personal power

- identify that anytime they claim "you made me do it" as a way of explaining their feelings and behavior, they are avoiding responsibility

- identify that other people's actions or words might trigger a feeling or behavior, but that doesn't mean other people are responsible for that feeling or behavior

- understand that they are responsible for their own feelings and behavior
- discover one new way to stick up for themselves when they make mistakes
- identify the Happiness List as a way to begin collecting and storing good feelings to help them develop personal power

MATERIALS

- an object that illustrates a wall or barrier; a sign that says "You Made Me Do It!" [activity 2]
- copies of the "Questions for Role Play" handout (page 34) [activity 2]
- copies of the student book, *Stick Up for Yourself!* [activities 3, 6]
- chalkboard or flip chart [activity 5]
- student notebooks [activities 5, 6]
- copies of the "How to Keep a Happiness List" handout (page 35) [activity 6]

AGENDA

1. Introduce the session.
2. Lead the role play "You Made Me Do It."
3. Give students time to read pages 8–15 and 86–90 (starting with "How to Live Happily Ever After") in the student book, if they haven't already done so.
4. Lead a discussion about how other people trigger our reactions.
5. Lead the activity "Nobody's Perfect" and ask students to write at least one new way they will deal with their mistakes.
6. Introduce and explain the Happiness List. Give students time to write their happiness lists for today, and spend time discussing their reactions.
7. Close the session and assign the reading for Session 3.

ACTIVITIES . . . .

1. INTRODUCTION

Say:

> Today you'll learn more about how to stick up for yourself.
> One way to stick up for yourself is by getting and using
> personal power. Being responsible is an important part of
> personal power.
>
> Being responsible doesn't mean carrying the whole world on
> your shoulders, but it is a big job! In this session, you'll learn
> about what you're responsible for: *your own* behavior and *your*
> *own* feelings.

2. ROLE PLAY: "YOU MADE ME DO IT"

Ask:

> Has your doctor ever taken a little hammer and tapped it on the
> front part of your knee? What happened?
>
> Did you *make* your knee jerk, or did it just happen?
>
> We call that an *automatic response*. When someone does some-
> thing without thinking, it might be described as a "knee-jerk
> response." For a few minutes, we're going to talk about words
> many of us automatically say when something goes wrong and
> we don't want to be seen as responsible: "You made me do it!"
>
> Those words may be a sign that we're not being responsible for
> our behavior and feelings.

Show students an object in the room that suggests a barrier or wall.
Place the "You Made Me Do It" sign on it.

Say:

> The words "you made me do it" are like a wall we put up. We
> may do this automatically, like the knee-jerk response, or we
> may do it only now and then. Either way, whenever we say, "You
> made me do it," it's a sign that we're not being responsible.
>
> For fun, you're going to role-play in pairs. One person will ask a
> question. The other person will answer the question with what
> we're going to call a "you-made-me-do-it" answer.

You won't use the words "you made me do it," but that's the message you want to get across.

Here's an example:

The question is: "Why didn't you take out the garbage?"

A "you-made-me-do-it" answer is: "You didn't put it by the back door, so I didn't know it needed to go out."

Can you think of another "you-made-me-do-it" answer for this question?

If they can't think of any, you might suggest one or more of the following:

- You didn't tell me it was full.

- You never said that was my job this week.

- You didn't sort the stuff for recycling.

- You didn't get me up early enough, so I didn't have time.

When you're sure the class has the idea, divide them into pairs (or into groups of three or four, if that works better).

Hand out copies of "Questions for Role Play."

Ask students to try to think of at least one "you-made-me-do-it" answer for each question. Tell them they'll only have a few minutes, so they need to work quickly. They can skip a question if they have trouble thinking of an answer.

Bring the groups back together again, but have them stay in the same area with their small group. Ask one of the questions. Go from group to group, asking them to quickly give one answer they came up with in their group.

If appropriate, you might say:

It didn't seem that hard for you to come up with answers. I wonder if that means you're experts!

End the activity by saying:

Being responsible for your behavior and feelings can help you get and use personal power.

At one time or another, you may catch yourself saying to someone, "You made me do it!"

Saying "you made me do it" is a way we avoid being responsible.
It's a wall we put up that keeps us from getting and using
personal power.

Whenever you hear yourself say, "You made me do it," remind
yourself: "No one else is responsible for my behavior or feelings.
No one made me do it."

3. READING

Ask students to quickly review pages 8–15 in *Stick Up for Yourself!*
Tell them to close their books when they're done so you'll be able to
tell they're ready to go on. Then ask:

If someone talks you into doing something, are you responsible
for your behavior?

If you do something without thinking—you just do it—are you
responsible? Why or why not? When has this happened to you?

If you do something you really didn't mean to do, are you
responsible? Why or why not? When has this happened to you?

Can someone else make you feel angry or sad or happy? Why or
why not?

If students have trouble with this question, remind them of the
point by saying:

What other people say or do may trigger your feelings, but they
didn't make you feel that way. You are responsible for your own
feelings.

Say:

Turn to page 14 in *Stick Up for Yourself!* Find what the authors say
is the main reason for being responsible. When you find it, raise
your hand.

Ask someone to read aloud what they found:

The main reason is because it's the best thing to do for you. Being
responsible helps you feel secure and confident inside yourself. It
gives you a feeling of *personal power.*

Say:

> It may take time before you're really comfortable with the fact that you're responsible for your own behavior and feelings.
>
> Change takes time.
>
> Changing the way you think about things is like wearing a new pair of shoes. Sometimes it takes a while before new shoes are comfortable to walk in. They may even pinch your feet. If you keep wearing them, they start to feel more comfortable and natural—a part of you.
>
> Keep in mind that being responsible is a way to get and use personal power.

4. TRIGGERS

Ask:

> Have you ever said to someone, "I knew you would say that!" or "I knew you would do that!" Can you give me an example?
>
> How did you know what they were going to do or say?

Lead the discussion until someone expresses the idea that we know what they're going to do or say because we've seen them react that way in similar situations. Then ask:

> How many of you know something you could say to someone, and then they would cry or get angry? Why do you feel so sure about that?

Help students see that we begin to predict someone's behavior because 1) we've seen them react in a similar situation, and 2) we know what's important to them. Then say:

> Even though you're responsible only for your own behavior, sometimes your behavior might trigger a behavior or feeling in another person.
>
> Here are two examples:
>
> - You didn't *make* your friend cry. But when you didn't ask her to your party, she felt sad. Not getting an invitation was a trigger for her sadness.
>
> - Your brother didn't *make* you angry. But when he spilled paint on your new shirt, it was a trigger for your anger.

Ask:

> If your mom always gets angry when you leave dirty dishes on the floor in your room, are you responsible for her feeling angry?
>
> Are the dirty dishes a trigger?
>
> Do you think that leaving dirty dishes on the floor would be a trigger if you had never done this before? Is it more likely to be a trigger if you have done it many times before?

Tell everyone to pair up with a person nearby. Then say:

> Take turns. First, tell about something you do that triggers a feeling or behavior in someone else. Then tell about something another person does that triggers a reaction in you. First something you do; then something another person does.

After two or three minutes, bring the class back together and ask:

> Would anyone like to share what you do that triggers a reaction in someone else?
>
> Did anyone think of something another person does that triggers an angry feeling in you? A hurt feeling? A happy feeling? An excited feeling? A scared feeling? An ashamed feeling?
>
> Can you think of one way that being aware of triggers can help you?

5. NOBODY'S PERFECT

Ask:

> Has anyone here ever made a mistake?
>
> Raise your hand if you've made one mistake.
>
> Is there anyone who has made two mistakes? Three? More than three? More than you can count?
>
> Who is the Mistake Champion of our class/group?

If appropriate, you might say:

> I'm sure I've got you beat. You haven't lived as long as I have.

Ask:

> Now, is there anyone here who thinks they're never going to make another mistake?
>
> Who would like to think they're not going to make the same mistakes?

Say:

> You're going to make mistakes. It's part of life.
>
> Being responsible means you don't blame someone else for your mistakes. You admit your mistakes and learn from them.
>
> It matters what you tell yourself when you make a mistake. You can help or hurt your self-esteem.

Ask:

> What do you tell yourself when you make a mistake?
>
> Do you know what it means to forgive yourself?

Write on the chalkboard or flip chart:

> When I make a mistake, I usually tell myself…
> From now on, when I make a mistake I'm going to tell myself…

Ask students to open their notebooks. Say:

> In your notebook, copy and finish the sentences I've written here.

End the activity by saying:

> Every human being has the right to make mistakes every day. That includes you.

6. THE HAPPINESS LIST

Say:

> Turn to a clean page in your notebook.

Ask:

> Has anybody ever told you that you're a collector? What did they mean?

Say:

> Some people collect lots of things, and the spaces where they live or work or go to school become packed with things. We do this with feelings, too. We collect feelings. And those collected feelings become part of a bigger and bigger collection.
>
> It's important to have lots of good feelings in your collection.
>
> Remembering good feelings is one way you help yourself feel secure and confident, no matter what!
>
> Collecting and storing feelings can help you get and use personal power—if your collection is made up of good feelings.
>
> Pages 87 through 90 in your book talk about the Happiness List. Turn to page 89 and follow along as I read the five reasons it's so important to keep a Happiness List every day:

1. It boosts your *personal power*.
2. It teaches you that *you are responsible* for your own happiness.
3. It teaches you that *you can choose* how to experience your life.
4. It teaches you to look for things that *create* happiness.
5. It teaches you how to *collect and store* good feelings.

Say:

> Today we're going to start keeping a Happiness List, and we'll do this for the rest of the course. Or maybe for the rest of our lives! Who knows—maybe we could end up with the biggest collection of good feelings in the history of the world!
>
> These don't have to be Big Things. Noticing small things can make us happy, too. Start to notice what makes you smile. Those are the things you want to put on your list. Let's get started.
>
> Right now, write down five things that happened today—things you feel good about that put a smile on your face.

Give students time to write. Then ask:

> Was this easy for you to do, or hard? Does anyone want to tell how they felt about doing this?
>
> Anyone else?

Say:

> **There are four simple steps you can follow to keep a Happiness List and collect lots of good feelings.**

Hand out copies of "How to Keep a Happiness List." Read it to the students or ask them to read:

1. STOP everything and notice what's making you happy, then
2. FEEL the happy feeling, then
3. STORE it inside of you, then
4. WRITE it down as soon as you can.

End the activity by saying:

> **For the rest of the course, keep a Happiness List every day. Start your collection and watch it grow.**
>
> **In future sessions, we'll talk more about the Happiness List. For now, just get started.**

7. CLOSING

Summarize by saying:

> **In this session, we learned that we are responsible for our own behavior and feelings. We are *not* responsible for other people's feelings or behavior—only our own.**
>
> **One way to be more responsible is to stop saying "you made me do it."**
>
> **We also learned about triggers. Sometimes our behavior triggers certain feelings or behaviors in other people. But we didn't *make* them feel or act that way. They are responsible for their behavior and feelings, just as we are responsible for our own.**
>
> **Sometimes other people's behavior triggers certain feelings or reactions in us, but they didn't *make* us feel or act that way. We are responsible for our behavior and feelings, just as they are responsible for their own.**
>
> **Everyone makes mistakes. It's important to expect to make mistakes every day. It's also important to forgive ourselves when we make mistakes.**

One way to get and use personal power is to collect good feelings. Keeping a Happiness List will help us do that.

In the next session, we'll begin talking about another important part of developing personal power: making choices.

Say:

Before the next session, read pages 16 through 20 in *Stick Up for Yourself!*

If necessary, tell students where and when the next session will be.

QUESTIONS FOR ROLE PLAY

 Where is your homework?

Why didn't you call like you said you would?

Why did you wear my sweater without asking?

What happened to the change
from the $5 I gave you?

Why are you late to class?

Why aren't the dishes washed?

Who broke this?

Tell me why your grades dropped.

HOW TO KEEP A HAPPINESS LIST

Whenever something happens that puts a smile on your face:

1. **STOP** everything and notice what's making you happy, then

2. **FEEL** the happy feeling, then

3. **STORE** it inside of you, then

4. **WRITE** it down as soon as you can.

Try to do this five times every day. Weekdays and weekends. School days and holidays. Be happy five times every day.

SESSION THREE
MAKING CHOICES

OVERVIEW . . . .

Stick Up for Yourself!
Reading Assignment
pages 16–20

In this session, students develop an understanding of the statement "Because you are responsible for your own behavior and feelings, you can make choices about them."

Students learn the importance of identifying and making choices. Activities help them learn to separate feelings from acting on feelings. Although they have some choices regarding how they feel, they have more choices in what to do about the feeling.

The relationship between expectations and feelings is discussed. To determine what their expectations are, students can learn to ask, "What do I hope will happen? What are the chances it will happen?" Having realistic expectations helps them develop personal power.

LEARNER OUTCOMES . . . .

The purpose of this session is to help students:

- understand that they can choose how to feel
- understand that they can choose what to do about a feeling
- identify realistic and unrealistic expectations
- identify ways in which their feelings and their expectations are sometimes tied together

MATERIALS . . . .

- copies of the student book, *Stick Up for Yourself!* [activity 2]
- chalkboard or flip chart [activity 4]
- student notebooks [activity 5]

36

AGENDA . . . .

1. Introduce the session.

2. Give students time to read pages 16–20 in the student book, if they haven't already done so, and have a brief discussion.

3. Lead the activity "Choices." *Optional:* Conclude this activity with a role play.

4. Lead the activity "What Do You Expect?" to help students identify realistic and unrealistic expectations.

5. Lead the activity "Becoming More Realistic" to develop students' understanding of how expectations influence feelings.

6. Close the session and assign the reading for Session 4.

ACTIVITIES . . . .

1. INTRODUCTION

Say:

> **This session is about choices you can make in how you feel and act.**
>
> **How many of you often say or think, "I didn't have a choice"?**
>
> **Sometimes you're right. You don't always have a choice about something you have to do. But sometimes you overlook choices. This session will help you begin to notice the choices you have.**
>
> **Identifying choices and making good ones are things you can do to stick up for yourself.**

2. READING

Ask students to read or review pages 16–20 in *Stick Up for Yourself!* Tell them to close their books when they're done so you'll be able to tell they're ready to go on. Then say:

> **In your book, you read about Maria, who got a math test back from her teacher. The teacher had written, "You can do better!" Imagine yourself in that situation for a minute. How would you feel?**
>
> **Maria could feel angry or bad about herself. Or she could decide that what she did was good enough. That is a way to stick up for herself.**

Who has had an experience like Daniel? When you needed to talk to someone right away, but you couldn't get the person's attention for one reason or another? How did you feel? Why do you think you felt that way? What did you do? What else could you have done?

Being able to identify choices we have about our feelings and our actions gives us personal power.

3. CHOICES

Say:

We're going to take a few minutes to listen to a story and practice identifying possible choices that a boy named Joseph has.

Ask the class to listen as you read the following. (You may need to read the story more than once.)

Joseph is at a friend's apartment. His mom wants him home by 8 P.M. sharp. That means he needs to catch the 7:30 bus.

Joseph stays too long at his friend's place and misses the bus. The next one comes at 8:00—but he won't get home until 8:30, a half-hour late.

He could take the subway at 7:45 and still make it home by 8:00—but his mom has told him never to ride the subway after 7:00.

Stop the story and ask:

What choices does Joseph have?

Allow time for discussion. Students may pick up on the fact that regardless of what Joseph decides, he's going to break one of his mom's rules. Either he takes the bus and arrives home late, or he takes the subway when he's not allowed.

Continue the story:

Joseph tries calling his mom, but there's no answer. He decides to take the bus and be late.

Stop the story and ask:

What do you think of the choice Joseph made? Why?

Continue the story:

> When Joseph gets off the bus at his stop, his mom is there waiting for him. She doesn't look happy.

Stop the story and ask:

> **What choices does Joseph have now? In what he feels? In how he acts?**

Continue the story:

> The first thing his mom says is, "You're half an hour late. You're grounded!"

Ask:

> **What do you think Joseph is feeling right now?**
>
> **What choices does he have right now in how he feels or acts?**
>
> **What could he say or do that might help the situation?**
>
> **What could he say or do that would make the situation worse?**

NOTE: You may either conclude the activity at this point or do a brief role play. If you're ending the activity now, say:

> **We can't always predict what choices we're going to have to make. Sometimes we make good choices, sometimes not so good.**
>
> **We gain personal power when we learn to recognize—on the spot—the choices that are ours to make.**

OPTIONAL: ROLE PLAY

Ask:

> **Has anyone here ever come home later than you were supposed to?**

Ask the class to divide into pairs. In each pair, ask the person whose first name starts with the letter closest to the front of the alphabet to play the role of the parent. Ask the other person to play the role of the child.

Say:

> Here's the situation: If you're the child, you're just walking into your home. You're an hour late, and your parent is waiting for you.
>
> Take a couple of minutes to decide two things: 1) how you're going to act, and 2) how you're going to let us know what you're feeling.

Bring the class back together and ask for volunteers to begin the role play. Afterward, ask the class:

> Did you have any trouble figuring out what each person was feeling?
>
> Was there a place where either person seemed to make a choice?

Ask for volunteers for one more role play. Say:

> This time, I want you to act out the scene without using words.

After the role play, ask the class:

> Did you have any trouble figuring out what they were feeling?

End the activity by saying:

> We have choices in how we act and how we feel.
>
> We gain personal power when we learn to recognize—on the spot—the choices that are ours to make.

4. WHAT DO YOU EXPECT?

Say:

> Sometimes we set ourselves up for disappointment. One way we do this is by hoping something will happen that isn't likely to happen.

Write on the chalkboard or flip chart:

R_x for Disappointment:
We hope something will happen that isn't likely to happen.

When we don't get what we hope for, we may become angry or sad. We might even feel that it's somehow our fault. In this activity, we're going to practice identifying the kinds of things we may hope for that set us up for disappointment.

Give this example:

What if I tell myself, "I'm going to smile at you more often, because if I smile, it will make you all feel very happy"?

What do I expect to happen because I smile? Do you think that is a realistic expectation? Is it likely to happen? *(No, it is not realistic.)*

What if I tell myself, "I'm going to smile at you more often so you'll be able to see how much I enjoy being with you"? Is that a realistic expectation? Is it likely that my smiling will let you know I like being with you?

Choose three of the following sentences (or others you feel may be more relevant to your group) and write them on the chalkboard or flip chart:

If I grow two inches taller…
If I change my hair…
If I lose ten pounds…
If I gain ten pounds…
If I get in with the right group…
When I leave home…
When I have a boyfriend/girlfriend, my life will be…
If I go to a different school next year…

Divide the class into groups of two or three. Then say:

Each group will make up endings for the sentences on the board—but some groups will do *realistic* endings, and others will do endings that are *not realistic*.

Go around to each group and whisper to them whether they are to make up realistic or unrealistic endings.

After a few minutes, bring the groups back together. Read the first sentence. Ask one of the small groups to read aloud the ending they wrote. Then ask the rest of the class:

Was that a realistic or unrealistic ending? Why do you think so?

The unrealistic endings should be obvious. Some of the realistic endings may seem debatable, and you'll need to allow some discussion. Move on before the discussion begins to drag.

Continue until each group has had at least one chance to contribute. End the activity when it's clear that the class understands the difference between realistic and unrealistic expectations. Then ask:

> **Who can summarize for us how realistic expectations influence feelings?**

5. BECOMING MORE REALISTIC

Say:

> **I want you to think of something that happens in your life that always makes you feel angry or sad. Think about that feeling for a minute.**
>
> **Turn to a clean page in your notebook. I'm going to read three sentence starters. I want you to finish each sentence, describing the feeling you're thinking about right now.**

Read each of the following sentence starters, pausing for a moment after each one to give students time to write:

> I think I feel that way because…
> What I always hope will happen is…
> The chances it will happen are…

Say:

> **Now I want you to think of something that happens in your life that always makes you feel happy. Think about that feeling for a minute.**
>
> **In your notebook, finish these sentences, describing the feeling you're thinking about right now:**
>
> - **"I think I feel that way because…"**
>
> - **"What I always hope will happen is…"**
>
> - **"The chances it will happen are…"**

Ask:

> **In the situations you wrote about, is it possible that your feelings had a lot to do with what you hoped or expected would happen?**
>
> **Would anyone like to share your thoughts with us?**

End the activity by saying:

> **Start being more aware of times when you feel angry or sad. When it happens, ask yourself, "What was I expecting?" This may help you figure out whether or not you have realistic expectations for yourself and other people.**

6. CLOSING

Summarize by saying:

> **In this session, you learned that part of sticking up for yourself is making choices, on the spot, about how to feel or act.**
>
> **Sometimes you may feel disappointed or angry or sad because your expectations are not realistic.**
>
> **Having realistic expectations can help you develop more personal power.**

Say:

> **Before the next session, read pages 21 through 45 in *Stick Up for Yourself!* (through "Talk About Your Feelings"). The next time we meet, we'll talk about feelings and learn how to give them names. This is a longer than usual reading assignment, so please make sure to read it ahead of time.**

If necessary, tell students where and when the next session will be.

SESSION FOUR
NAMING YOUR FEELINGS

OVERVIEW . . . .

Stick Up for Yourself!
Reading Assignment
pages 21–45 (through
"Talk About
Your Feelings")

In this session, students learn to name their feelings. They discover that one part of getting to know themselves is calling feelings by their right names. This is a vital session, because students' personal power is very often dependent on whether they are able to name (then claim or own) the feeling they are having. Activities and discussions develop the understanding that the body's reaction helps us identify a feeling.

LEARNER OUTCOMES . . . .

The purpose of this session is to help students:

- understand that part of sticking up for themselves is knowing what they are feeling

- identify and name feelings

- understand that knowing names for feelings makes it easier to communicate what they are feeling

MATERIALS . . . .

- copies of the student book, *Stick Up for Yourself!* [activities 2, 3]

- slips of paper, each with the name of one low-intensity feeling written on it (see student book page 25) [activity 3]

- *Optional:* slips of paper with the names of combined feelings written on them (see student book pages 39–44) [activity 3]

- chalkboard or flip chart [activity 4]

- student notebooks [activity 5]

AGENDA . . . .

1. Introduce the session.
2. Review one part of the reading assignment and tell how the reading will be used in this session.

3. Review another part of the reading assignment and lead the role play "Name That Feeling." *Optional:* Expand the readings and role play to include combined feelings.

4. Lead the discussion "What Your Body Is Telling You" to help students learn to notice how their bodies can help them name their feelings.

5. Lead the activity "Recipe for a Good Feeling" to help students identify "ingredients" that might result in a certain feeling.

6. Close the session and assign the reading for Session 5.

ACTIVITIES ....

1. INTRODUCTION

Say:

> **In earlier sessions, we learned two ways to get personal power: 1) being responsible for your feelings and behavior, and 2) making choices.**
>
> **Today we're going to begin talking about a third way to get personal power: getting to know yourself. An important part of knowing yourself is knowing what you're feeling. This session is about naming your feelings.**

2. READING

Have students turn to pages 22–23 in *Stick Up for Yourself!* Tell them to follow along silently while you read aloud the last two paragraphs on 22 and the first paragraph on 23:

> Feelings have their own special names. The more names you know, the more you can understand your feelings and tell other people about them. And the more you can stick up for yourself.
>
> Names are like handles for our feelings. Knowing the right name for a feeling allows us to "pick it up," learn about it, and make choices about it.
>
> Calling feelings by their right names adds to your personal power. Calling feelings by their wrong names takes away from your personal power.

Say:

> We're not going to take time right now to read or review all the pages on feelings. Instead, we'll be reading parts as we do the activities in this session.

3. NAME THAT FEELING

Ask:

> Has anyone ever asked you, "How do you feel about what happened?" and you couldn't think of an answer?
>
> Before we can tell someone about what we're feeling—or even describe it to ourselves—it helps to have a name for the feeling.
>
> Turn to page 25. We're going to take a few minutes to talk about the nine low-intensity feelings listed at the bottom of the page.
>
> Let's start with *interest.* I'd like someone to volunteer to read the first paragraph on page 26, which tells about *interest.* Stop when you get to "Things (and people)...."

Follow this procedure until you have gone through all nine feelings on the low-intensity list: *interest, enjoyment, surprise, fear, distress, anger, shame, dissmell, disgust.*

NOTE: Students should read only the descriptions of the feelings, not the lists of things/times/events that might evoke the feelings. For some of the readings, you may need to tell students where to start and stop. Here are the readings:

INTEREST (page 26): When you're *interested* in something, you're curious about it. It holds your attention. You concentrate on it. You want to know more about it. When you're interested in a person, you're fascinated by him or her.

ENJOYMENT (page 27): When you're *enjoying* yourself, you're smiling and feeling good.

SURPRISE (page 29): When you're *surprised* by something, you may not know how to act at first. You weren't expecting what happened, so you're not sure what to do. Maybe you don't say or do anything for a moment or two. You need time to process the experience.

FEAR (page 30): When you're *fearful,* you're worried and afraid. You think something bad is about to happen, or someone is about to threaten or hurt you.

DISTRESS (page 31): When you're *distressed* about something, you feel sad about it, and sometimes you cry.

ANGER (page 33): Anger can be sudden and fierce, here in a moment and gone in a flash. Or it can start slowly and build, then burn for a long time. You might feel *angry* at a particular person or about a particular thing. Or you might feel angry at everyone and everything.

SHAME (page 35): When you're *shamed*, you feel exposed. You want to run and hide or cover yourself up. It feels like everyone suddenly knows you're just no good. Or like something is wrong with you inside, and everyone can see it.

DISSMELL (page 37): When you *experience dissmell*, it's usually because something or someone close to you suddenly smells very bad and you have to pull away quickly. Dissmell is our natural response to bad odors.

DISGUST (page 38): When you're *disgusted* with someone, you can hardly stand to be around that person. You feel as if that person makes you sick. You feel like getting rid of that person, the way you would spit something out. It's also possible to feel disgusted with yourself.

Say:

Now let's do a role play. I'm going to divide you into small groups. Each group will get a slip of paper with the name of a feeling written on it.

Your group has to figure out how to show us the feeling—without using any words. You can't talk about it; you can only act it out.

Decide as a group whether everyone in the group will do the same thing, or if you'll each do something different. Remember, you can't tell us the name of the feeling. You have to show us.

If you can't figure out what to do, reread the part of your book that talks about that feeling.

Any questions? (*Answer any questions they have.*)

Divide the class into groups of two, three, or four, depending on the size of your class. You'll need at least nine groups. Give each group a slip of paper with the name of the feeling they are to act out.

Allow practice time, then call the groups together and point to one group to begin.

After the group shows the feeling, ask the others:

What feeling are they acting out?

Why do you think so?

What helped you decide? Was anything confusing?

Continue until each group has had a chance to contribute. End by saying:

In this activity, we practiced naming feelings based on what we saw. Nonverbal behavior helped us "read" and name feelings.

OPTIONAL: COMBINED FEELINGS

If time allows, expand the readings and role play to include the combined feelings described on pages 39–44 of the student book. You might start by asking:

Who can tell me what happens when you mix red and blue together? *(They combine to make purple.)* **What about when you mix blue and yellow?** *(Green.)* **Red and yellow?** *(Orange.)*

The nine feelings we just learned about are like colors. Sometimes they combine. When they do, they create more feelings. These feelings have names, too.

Read aloud the following descriptions of the four combined feelings discussed in the student book:

CONTEMPT (page 40): To feel *contemptuous* is to look down on other people. You think you're better than they are. You feel as if there's something wrong with them, and they don't deserve to be liked or respected. Contempt is a combination of *anger* and *dissmell*.

JEALOUSY (pages 41–42): To feel *jealous* is to feel bad inside because someone else has something you want. Or suddenly you have a rival for someone else's affections or attention. You feel less worthy or inferior—like there's something wrong with you. At the same time, you feel angry and resentful. Jealousy is a combination of *shame* and *anger*.

LONELINESS (pages 42–43): To feel *lonely* is to feel like an outsider. You want to feel close to someone, or you want to belong to a group, but instead you feel shut out, ignored, and unwanted. It seems that no one understands you, wants to be with you, or cares about you. Loneliness is a combination of *shame* and *distress*.

DOWN MOOD (pages 43–44): When your mood is up, you feel excited or joyful. When your mood is *down*, your head hangs low, your shoulders sag, and you might feel like crying. Some people use the word "depressed" to describe a down mood, but depression is different and more serious. Like loneliness, a down mood is a combination of *shame* and *distress*.

Include the combined feelings in the role play. Depending on the size of your class, you might need to have some small groups act out more than one feeling.

4. WHAT YOUR BODY IS TELLING YOU

Before you begin this activity, write on the chalkboard or flip chart the names of the seven high-intensity feelings listed on page 25 of the student book:

Excitement
Joy
Startle
Terror
Anguish
Rage
Humiliation

NOTE: Dissmell and disgust are included among the low-intensity feelings listed on page 25 of the student book, but they can also be high-intensity. You might want to add them to this discussion.

Say:

You can learn a lot about your feelings by listening to what your body is telling you.

Think about the last time you were really angry—so angry you were full of rage. How does it feel to be *enraged*? Where in your body do you feel rage?

Write their answers beside *rage* on the list. Their answers might include: I clench my fists; my face gets hot; I feel like screaming.

What about *terror*? How does your body help you know you're terrified?

Write their answers beside *terror* on the list. Their answers might include: I can't move (frozen stiff); my stomach feels tight; my hands get cold; I'm extra alert and watchful; I'm nervous; my body shakes; my knees shake; my teeth chatter; I'm sweating.

What about *startle*? How does your body let you know you're startled?

Write their answers beside *startle* on the list. Their answers might include: I yell out loud; I jump; I put my hands up to my chest; I cover my eyes with my hands.

Continue until you have written at least one or two bodily or facial reactions beside each of the seven words on the list.

End the activity by saying:

While you're learning to name your feelings, it helps to tune in to what your body is telling you. You experience feelings not only in your mind but also in your body.

With practice, you'll get better at naming your feelings. Knowing what you're feeling can help you know what to do about the feeling.

5. RECIPE FOR A GOOD FEELING

Say:

For fun, let's make up a recipe for a good feeling.

We know the amounts of each ingredient, but we don't know what the ingredients are. Let's start with *joy*. Each ingredient has to be something that might bring about that feeling.

Write the following recipe starter on the chalkboard or flip chart:

> JOY
>
> 1 quart of _____
> 1 cup of _____
> 2 tablespoons of _____
> 1/2 teaspoon of _____
> dash of _____
>
> Bake for _____

Say:

> **Here's what we know so far. *(Point to the recipe and read what you have written.)* Now let's finish the recipe.**

Write students' suggestions on the board next to the ingredients. If students have trouble getting the idea, give this example:

> 1 quart of Saturday afternoon
> 1 cup of good friends
> 2 tablespoons of funny jokes
> 1/2 teaspoon of snacks
> dash of sunshine
>
> Bake for 2 hours

When the students' recipe is finished, have someone read it aloud.

Say:

> **Turn to a clean page in your notebook and write your own recipe for a good feeling you would like to have more often. You might write a recipe for joy, interest, excitement, enjoyment, or surprise.**
>
> **If you want, you can look at pages 26 through 29 in *Stick Up for Yourself!* and find more names for these good feelings. Look under the "Get Personal" boxes for lists of more names. You may call your feeling any name you want.**

Give students time to write their recipes. Then ask:

> **Does anyone have a recipe they'd like to share?**

Say:

> **Just read your ingredients. Let us see if we can figure out what the feeling is.**

End the activity by saying:

> **There's more than one recipe for joy *(or interest, excitement, etc.).* But if we stop and think about it, we can usually figure out why we feel a certain way. That gives us more information about our feeling, which adds to our personal power.**
>
> **Start being more aware of your feelings. When you notice a feeling, think about it for a few minutes. Ask yourself, "What's happening around me and inside me right now?" You'll learn more about what makes you feel mad, or sad, or glad.**

6. CLOSING

Summarize by saying:

> **In this session, you learned that naming your feelings is an important part of getting to know yourself.**
>
> **You learned that one way to name your feelings is to listen to what your body is telling you.**
>
> **When you're able to give your feeling the right name, you can choose what to do about it.**

Say:

> **Before the next session, read pages 57 through 71 in *Stick Up for Yourself!* (starting with "Claim Your Feelings, Future Dreams, and Needs"). The next time we meet, we'll talk about what it means to claim feelings, and you'll learn how to do it.**

If necessary, tell students where and when the next session will be.

SESSION FIVE
CLAIMING YOUR FEELINGS

OVERVIEW....................................

Stick Up for Yourself!
Reading Assignment
pages 57–71 (starting
with "Claim Your
Feelings, Future
Dreams, and Needs")

The primary goal of this session is to help students understand what it means to own a feeling (claim it as their own). Students learn that once they own a feeling, they can begin to identify choices they have in dealing with it. Talking things over with yourself is introduced as a way to help identify feelings and understand options. Students also learn ways to step outside of feelings at times when their feelings are too powerful to deal with.

LEARNER OUTCOMES....................................

The purpose of this session is to help students:

- understand that part of sticking up for themselves is claiming (owning) their feelings

- understand how talking things over with themselves can help them learn more about their feelings

- identify ways to detach from or let go of feelings that are too strong to cope with at the moment

- identify positive ways to deal with strong feelings

MATERIALS....................................

- copies of the student book, *Stick Up for Yourself!* [activities 2, 3, 4, 5]

- chalkboard or flip chart [activity 3]

- slips of paper, one for each student, and a sack to put them in [activity 3]

- copies of the "Talk Things Over with Yourself (Talk About Feelings)" handout (page 63) [activity 4]

- student notebooks [activity 6]

- extra copies of the "Session Topics and Reading Assignments" handout (page 13) [activity 7]

AGENDA . . . .

1. Introduce the session.

2. Review the reading assignment.

3. Lead the activity "What Does It Mean to Claim a Feeling?" and briefly discuss ways to avoid claiming a feeling.

4. Lead the activity "Talking Things Over with Yourself" to help students learn more about a feeling, on the spot, by having a conversation with themselves.

5. Lead the activity "Great Escapes" to help students identify their choices when a feeling is too strong to handle at the moment.

6. Lead the activity "Dealing with Strong Feelings" to help students recognize that there are positive ways to handle strong feelings and adults they can talk to about their feelings.

7. Close the session and assign the reading for Session 6.

ACTIVITIES . . . .

1. INTRODUCTION

Say:

> In this session, we'll continue talking about feelings. During the last session, you learned to *name* your feelings. This session is about *claiming* your feelings.
>
> Naming and claiming your feelings helps you get to know yourself and builds your personal power.

2. READING

Ask students to read or review pages 57–58 in *Stick Up for Yourself!*, starting with "Claim Your Feelings, Future Dreams, and Needs." Tell them to raise their hands when they're done but to keep their books open. Then ask:

> What do the authors say about locking up feelings inside yourself or trying to push them away? Let's find that part and read it again.

Students should locate the last two paragraphs on page 58. Ask a volunteer to read them aloud:

> You may try to push away some feelings, future dreams, and needs, or lock them up inside yourself. This isn't a good idea, because they don't stay away or hidden. They can turn into problems later.
>
> Many adults today have problems in their lives. Doctors and psychologists think it's because they denied or buried important feelings, future dreams, and needs when they were kids. When we do this, we lose track of who we are. We lose our *selves*.

Say:

In this session, you'll learn about claiming your feelings instead of pushing them away or locking them up inside yourself. We'll learn about naming and claiming future dreams later on in this course.

3. WHAT DOES IT MEAN TO CLAIM A FEELING?

Say:

Let's take a couple of minutes to see if we can remember the names of feelings we talked about during the last session. Without looking in your book, can you think of one? Another one? Any more?

As students name the feelings, list them on the chalkboard or flip chart. They may name all of the feelings, but if they don't, say:

Now look back at page 25 in your book. Which feelings did we miss?

Continue until you've listed all of the low-intensity and high-intensity feelings on the chalkboard or flip chart. Then say:

We also learned the names of four combined feelings. Can anyone remember what they are? *(Contempt, jealousy, loneliness, down mood.)*

Add those feelings to the list. Then say:

In the last session, we learned that it's important to know the names of feelings. This makes it easier for us to talk about what we're feeling and do something about it.

It also makes it easier for us to claim our feelings.

Think about how you're feeling right now. What is the name of your feeling? Maybe it's one of the feelings listed on the board. Or maybe none of those words describes exactly how you feel.

If you want, take a few moments to look at pages 25 through 44 in *Stick Up for Yourself!* The authors have listed more names and opposites for each of the feelings. Maybe one of those names works better for you.

Once you have a name for your feeling, come to the front of the room, take a slip of paper out of the sack, and write your feeling name on the paper. Then take it with you and return to your seat.

Allow time for students to complete this part of the activity. Then say:

Guess what? All of you just claimed your feeling. You thought about how you were feeling. You named your feeling. You wrote it down and you have it now. It's yours.

Claiming a feeling isn't that hard. In fact, it's easier than the things people sometimes do to *avoid* claiming a feeling. Let's talk about some of those things and why they don't work.

Write on the chalkboard or flip chart:

WAYS TO AVOID CLAIMING A FEELING

Push it away.
Lock it up inside yourself.
Question it.
Judge it.
Ignore it.
Call it by some other name.

Lead a brief discussion about each item on this list. Don't dwell too long on any item. The point is to help students see that none is an effective way to deal with feelings. Start by asking:

What happens when you try to push a feeling away? Is it even possible? Can you push away feeling afraid, or angry, or jealous? Will the feeling stay away?

What about when you lock up a feeling inside yourself? In the last session, we talked about how you can learn about your feelings by listening to what your body is telling you. Do you think it helps or hurts your body if you lock your feelings inside?

What about when you question a feeling? Like "Hey, anger! What are you doing here?" Is that a good way to do something about the feeling? Why or why not?

Does it help to judge a feeling? What if you decide, "This is a bad feeling" or "This is a good feeling"? Look at page 24 of your book to see what the authors say about this. When you find it, raise your hand.

Have a volunteer read aloud these sentences from page 24 of the student book:

Feelings aren't wrong or right, bad or good. *Feelings just are.*

Ask:

Is it possible to ignore a feeling? Does that help? Why or why not?

What happens when we call a feeling by some other name instead of by its real name?

If students don't remember, direct them to the top of page 23 of their book. Have a volunteer read this sentence aloud:

Calling feelings by their wrong names takes away from your personal power.

Say:

Some of these ideas are a little hard to understand. Even grown-ups have trouble with them sometimes. So here's a fun way to remember them.

Imagine that your feeling is a brand-new puppy. It's *your* puppy, nobody else's.

Ask:

What happens if you try to push it away? Lock it up? Question it? Judge it? Ignore it? Call it by another name—like "kitty" or "goldfish"?

What's the best way to deal with your new puppy? *(Claim it!)*

End the activity by saying:

> When we claim a feeling, we name it and accept it fully. At that moment, it's part of us.

> Claiming a feeling doesn't mean we're stuck with it forever. It just means we know it's there and we own it.

4. TALKING THINGS OVER WITH YOURSELF

Say:

> You can learn a lot about your feelings by talking things over with yourself. Today we're going to practice doing that.

Hand out copies of "Talk Things Over with Yourself (Talk About Feelings)." Then say:

> Before you work on your own, let's look over the script on page 59 in *Stick Up for Yourself!* to get some ideas of how to do this.

> Notice that your "Talk Things Over with Yourself" sheet has the same questions as the script in the book, but there are blanks for you to fill in.

> Take a few minutes and write about what you're feeling right now, at this moment. Maybe it's the same feeling you claimed a few minutes ago, or maybe it's a different feeling.

> You won't have to share your writing with anyone else unless you want to. This is just for you.

> You might write about a feeling you'd like to change. Or you might write about a feeling you'd like to keep the way it is. Either is okay, as long as you write about what you're feeling right now.

After a few moments, ask:

> What did you learn from doing this?

> Did anyone have trouble figuring out what you were feeling?

> Does anyone want to share what you found out about your feeling?

> Did anyone have trouble figuring out what to do about your feeling?

> Does anyone want to share what you decided to do about your feeling?

Sometimes you can't change a feeling right away. It takes time. By talking things over with yourself, you may get some ideas about what to do about the feeling or what causes it.

End the activity by saying:

Keep this script in your notebook. It will help you remember the questions to ask when you want to talk feelings over with yourself.

5. GREAT ESCAPES

Say:

We've all had feelings that were so strong we didn't know what to do. After we claim a feeling, we may decide we want to leave it for now because it seems too strong to deal with at the moment.

On pages 61 through 64 of *Stick Up for Yourself!*, the authors talk about four Great Escapes. Turn to page 61 so we can quickly review what they are. Who can tell me what one of the four is? Another? A third? The fourth?

We're not going to talk about daydreaming in this course, but you may want to try it at home.

Someone here may already use one of these escapes.

Ask:

Does anyone use laughing as an escape? What do you find to laugh about?

Does anyone use exercise—like swimming or biking or running—to turn your attention away from a feeling? How well does it work for you? In what type of situations do you use it?

Say:

Sometimes we're in situations where we can't, right then, take a walk, or ride a bike, or find something to laugh about. It helps to have a way to escape a feeling, even when you can't escape the scene.

Let's learn a way right now.

Is there anyone in this room who has blown bubbles using a wand and bubble soap? Then you know how much fun it is to blow a really *big* bubble and watch it float away.

That's the idea behind a relaxation exercise we're about to do. Take a feeling you need to be away from, put it inside a bubble, and let it float away.

Even if you don't have a feeling right now that you want to escape, you might have something that's worrying you. We all have something we worry about, even if it's just now and then. You can use this exercise to get away from a worry.

Lead the students through the following relaxation exercise:

1. Sit comfortably in your chair, with your feet flat on the floor, and close your eyes.

2. Take a few deep breaths. Breathe in through your nose, and breathe out through your mouth.

3. Breathe in, breathe out. Breathe in, breathe out. Feel yourself relax.

4. Think for a minute about something that has been bothering you lately—it might be anything, big or small.

5. Picture yourself holding a huge bubble wand and a bottle of bubble soap. The bubble wand is as tall as you are, and the soap bottle takes up the whole corner of this room.

6. See yourself dipping the wand into the bottle.

7. Blow into the wand now. Watch a huge bubble start to form.

8. As the bubble forms, imagine your feeling or worry going inside the bubble. *(Pause for 10–15 seconds.)*

9. Watch the bubble float away, taking your worry with it. *(Pause.)*

10. Let it go. *(Pause.)*

11. Blow another bubble. Put another feeling or worry inside. *(Pause.)*

12. Watch it float away. *(Pause.)*

13. Let it go. *(Pause.)*

(Wait a minute or two, then say:)

14. Now take a deep breath, in through your nose, out through your mouth.

15. Feel what it's like to have your feeling or worry gone for now. Open your eyes again.

Conclude the relaxation exercise by saying:

Different people have different ways of letting go of feelings. The next time you have a feeling that's too strong to deal with at the moment, think about one way you can get away from it until it seems more manageable. Later, come back to it, and talk it over with yourself.

6. DEALING WITH STRONG FEELINGS

Say:

Taking a Great Escape isn't the same as pushing a feeling away, ignoring it, or any of the other things we talked about earlier. It's a way to take good care of ourselves until we're ready to handle the feeling.

Sooner or later, we have to deal with our feeling. Especially if it's a strong feeling—like fear, distress, anger, shame, jealousy, loneliness, or a down mood.

You might not be able to change a strong feeling right away. That takes time. But you don't have to let it run your life.

Pages 64 through 71 of *Stick Up for Yourself!* give you lots of ideas for handling strong feelings. Those pages were part of the reading assignment for today's session.

If you didn't read them yet, try to read them soon. You may want to read them more than once. Or, if you have one of the strong feelings named in the book, read that section first. You might want to copy some of the ideas into your notebook.

You'll notice that every section ends with the same idea: *Talk with an adult you trust.*

Say:

Turn to a clean page in your notebook. Write the name of an adult you trust and can talk to. This might be a parent, an aunt or uncle or grandparent, a grown-up brother or sister, a teacher, a school counselor, a coach, an adult leader at a club you belong to, a neighbor, or a religious leader.

After you write one name, write another, then another. Try to write the names of *three adults* you trust and can talk to.

Remember them the next time you need help dealing with a strong feeling.

7. CLOSING

Summarize by saying:

In this session, you learned that claiming your feelings is an important part of getting to know yourself.

You learned to talk things over with yourself and figure out what to do about a feeling.

When a feeling seems too strong to handle, you learned that you may need to let it go for a while. We talked about some Great Escapes you can do to let go of strong feelings until you're ready to deal with them.

You named at least one adult you trust and can talk to.

Say:

Before the next session, read pages 45 through 48 in *Stick Up for Yourself!* (starting with "Name Your Future Dreams"). Reread pages 57 through 60 (starting with "Claim Your Feelings, Future Dreams, and Needs"). Also read pages 97 through 100 (starting with "Keep an I-Did-It List").

These pages are listed on the "Session Topics and Reading Assignments" handout you received at the beginning of the course. If anyone needs an extra copy, let me know.

The next time we meet, we'll be talking about what it means to name and claim your dreams.

If necessary, tell students where and when the next session will be.

TALK THINGS OVER WITH YOURSELF
(TALK ABOUT FEELINGS)

Ask yourself, "How am I feeling today?" Then name a feeling you're having. Next, talk it over with yourself. Your talk might go like this:

SAY:

I'm feeling _____ today.

ASK:

Why am I feeling _____?

What's happened that I feel _____ about?

SAY:

I'm feeling _____

because _____

ASK:

What can I do about my _____ feeling?

SAY:

I can _____

_____

_____

SESSION SIX
NAMING AND CLAIMING YOUR DREAMS

OVERVIEW . . . .

Stick Up for Yourself!
Reading Assignment
pages 45–48 (starting
with "Name Your
Future Dreams"),
57–60 (starting with
"Claim Your Feelings,
Future Dreams, and
Needs"), and 97–100
(starting with "Keep
an I-Did-It List")

In this session, students learn another way to get personal power: by naming and claiming their dreams. The main concept presented here is that dreams are their personal goals. Dreams are important in developing personal power and positive self-esteem. Two kinds of dreams are discussed: near-future dreams and far-future dreams. Students learn how the two are related. They practice talking a dream over with themselves.

LEARNER OUTCOMES . . . .

The purpose of this session is to help students:

- understand that part of sticking up for yourself is naming and claiming dreams

- understand how talking things over with themselves can help them learn more about their dreams

- distinguish between near-future and far-future dreams

- identify the I-Did-It List as a way to build positive self-esteem

MATERIALS . . . .

- copies of the student book, *Stick Up for Yourself!* [activities 2, 5]

- chalkboard or flip chart [activity 3]

- student notebooks [activities 3, 6]

- volleyball and masking tape [activity 4]

- copies of the "Talk Things Over with Yourself (Talk About Dreams)" handout (page 74) [activity 5]

- extra copies of the "How to Keep a Happiness List" handout (page 35) [activity 6]

- copies of the "How to Keep an I-Did-It List" handout (page 75) [activity 6]
- extra copies of the "Session Topics and Reading Assignments" handout (page 13) [activity 7]

AGENDA . . . .

1. Introduce the session.
2. Review the reading assignment.
3. Lead the activity "Naming Your Dreams."
4. Lead the game "Dream Volley" to help students practice relating near-future and far-future dreams.
5. Lead the activity "Talking Things Over with Yourself" to help students learn to make choices about their dreams by having a conversation with themselves.
6. Lead the activity "The I-Did-It List."
7. Close the session and assign the reading for Session 7.

ACTIVITIES . . . .

1. INTRODUCTION

Say:

In this session, we'll talk about naming and claiming your dreams, which is a way to get to know yourself. It's also a way to get personal power.

2. READING

Ask students to read or review pages 45–48 in *Stick Up for Yourself!* (starting with "Name Your Future Dreams"). Tell them to close their books when they're done so you'll be able to tell they're ready to go on. Then ask:

Who can tell me why we need future dreams?

Give students a chance to answer the question. Then ask a volunteer to read the first paragraph under "Name Your Future Dreams" on page 45 of the student book:

Your future dreams are your personal goals. They give your life direction, purpose, and meaning. They guide your decisions and help you define the kind of person you are and want to be.

Ask:

Who can tell me how it affects us if we *don't* have future dreams?

Give students a chance to answer the question. Then ask a volunteer to read the second paragraph under "Name Your Future Dreams" on page 45 of the student book:

> What happens if you don't have future dreams? You have no personal goals. You have nothing to give your life direction, purpose, and meaning. You have nothing to guide your decisions and help you define the kind of person you are and want to be. You're like a car without a steering wheel, or a ship without a rudder. Future dreams are important!

Conclude the activity by saying:

In this session, you'll practice naming and claiming your dreams.

3. NAMING YOUR DREAMS

Say:

There are two kinds of dreams for you to think about: dreams for the *near future* and dreams for the *far future*. You need both kinds.

Let's figure out first what we mean by *near future* and *far future* so we're talking about the same thing. What do you think the *near future* is?

Discuss until you reach consensus.

What do you think the *far future* means? When you have finished your education or job training? When you're thirty or forty?

Discuss until you reach consensus.

I'd like to hear about some of your dreams for the far future. I'll tell you some of mine, too.

Write a list of dreams on the chalkboard or flip chart as students volunteer; include some of your own.

Now let's hear some of your dreams for the near future. I'll tell you some of mine, too.

Write a list of dreams on the chalkboard or flip chart as students volunteer; include some of your own.

> **Which list do you think has the "bigger dreams"—the far-future list or the near-future list? Does that make sense? Why or why not?**
>
> **Do you think our dreams for the far future and the near future need to be related? Why or why not?**

Say:

> **In your notebook, as quickly as you can, write down ten dreams you have. Don't think right now about whether they are for the far future or near future.**
>
> **You won't be asked to share these unless you want to. They are just for you to know about.**

Allow time for writing, then say:

> **Now, for each dream on your list, decide whether it's a near-future or far-future dream. Put an N beside each near-future dream and an F beside each far-future dream.**
>
> **Did you have both kinds of dreams on your list?**
>
> **Read one of your far-future dreams to yourself. Do you have a near-future dream to help make your far-future dream come true?**
>
> **Who has an example you'd be willing to share?**

End the activity by saying:

> **In this activity, we practiced naming our dreams. We learned that there are two kinds of dreams, far-future and near-future. We need both kinds.**

4. DREAM VOLLEY

Say:

> **It's not always easy to come up with near-future dreams related to our far-future dreams. We can imagine ourselves doing or being something in the future, but we're not sure how to get there.**
>
> **Let's get ideas from each other. We'll do this by playing a game called "Dream Volley."**

Clear an area of the room and position two teams as if they are on opposite sides of a net—a front row, a middle row, and a back row. The number of columns will depend on the size of your class. Indicate the net with a line of masking tape on the floor.

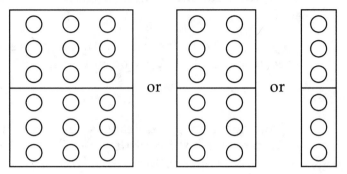

Say:

"Dream Volley" has some rules you have to learn, so listen carefully while I explain them. Then you'll have a chance to ask questions.

Point out the net (the masking tape). Then explain the rules:

Rule #1: In this game, you'll gently *toss* the ball to someone on the other side of the net, not hit it.

Rule #2: Before tossing the ball, you'll name a *far-future* dream—something you'd like to do or be someday.

Rule #3: When you catch the ball, you'll name a *near-future* dream related to the far-future dream of the person who tossed you the ball. So be sure to pay attention to two things: who tossed the ball, and what that person named as a far-future dream.

Rule #4: After you name a near-future dream, name a far-future dream of your own. Then toss the ball to someone else and listen to what that person says. He or she might have a good idea for a near-future dream for you.

Ask:

Does everyone understand what we'll be doing? Any questions?

Answer students' questions. If necessary, say:

Remember: You'll name *two* dreams. First is a near-future dream related to the other person's far-future dream. Next is a far-future dream of your own. When you toss the ball to someone

else, that person will name a near-future dream that might help you reach your far-future dream.

Let's practice before we start.

Name a far-future dream. (*Example:* "I want to sail around the world.") Toss the ball to a student. He or she should name a near-future dream related to your far-future dream. If the student has trouble doing this, offer a suggestion or two. (*Examples:* "I could read books about people who have sailed around the world. I could talk to someone who has done it. I could take sailing lessons.") Then have another student name a far-future dream and toss the ball to you. Name a near-future dream related to the student's far-future dream.

When the students seem ready, start the game. Allow them to play for 5–10 minutes, depending on their interest level. Every so often, you might want to interject a positive comment or two—like "Good idea!" or "Great dream!"

Afterward, have students return to their seats. Say:

We just heard a lot of ideas that can help us reach our dreams. Maybe there's an idea you'll want to try soon.

End the activity by saying:

It's important to have dreams. Dreams give your life direction, purpose, and meaning. It's important to have near-future dreams that will help you reach your far-future dreams.

5. TALKING THINGS OVER WITH YOURSELF

Say:

You can learn a lot about your dreams by talking things over with yourself. Today we're going to practice doing that.

Hand out copies of "Talk Things Over with Yourself (Talk About Dreams)." Then say:

Before you work on your own, let's look over the script on pages 59 and 60 in *Stick Up for Yourself!* to get some ideas of how to do this.

Notice that your "Talk Things Over with Yourself" sheet has the same questions as the script in the book, but there are blanks for you to fill in.

> Take a few minutes and write about a dream you have right now for the near future or far future. You won't have to share your dream with anyone else unless you want to. This is just for you.

After a few moments, ask:

> What did you learn from doing this?
>
> Did anyone have trouble figuring out what you have to learn to make your dream happen? By talking things over with yourself, you may get some ideas about what you need to learn.
>
> Does anyone want to share your dream and tell us what you decided to do to help make your dream come true?

Allow time for students who want to share. Then end the activity by saying:

> If you want, you can make a plan to start learning and doing things to make your dream happen. Write your plan in your notebook. You might plan to do one thing tomorrow, another thing next week, another thing by the end of the year, and so on. Whenever you learn or do something related to your dream, write it in your notebook.
>
> Keep this script in your notebook to help you remember the questions to ask when you want to talk dreams over with yourself.

6. THE I-DID-IT LIST

Say:

> In the second session, you learned how to keep a Happiness List to collect and store good feelings.
>
> Raise your hand if you've been keeping your Happiness List every day.

If all students raise their hands, congratulate them and move on. If some don't raise their hands, ask them to reread pages 86–90 of *Stick Up for Yourself!* when they get home (or later today, if there's time) and start keeping their list. Hand out extra copies of "How to Keep a Happiness List" to students who want or need them.

Say:

> Today you're going to begin keeping an I-Did-It List. It's like the Happiness List, but different.

Instead of writing down *things that happen* that put a smile on your face, you write down *things you do* that make you feel proud of yourself.

These might be activities you take part in. Problems you solve. Successes you achieve. Positive risks you take. Decisions you make. Challenges you meet. Goals you reach. People you help. Accomplishments of any kind. And anything else you feel satisfied with, good about, and proud of.

Like the Happiness List, the I-Did-It List boosts your personal power. It teaches you that you are responsible for feeling proud of yourself. You can choose to do things that make you feel proud. You can look for things to do that create a feeling of pride. You can collect and store proud feelings.

Turn to a clean page in your notebook. Right now, write down five things you did yesterday that you feel proud of. These don't have to be Big Things. Often you do good things when you're just being yourself.

Give students time to write. Then ask:

Did anyone get stuck trying to make a list? Maybe you were trying to think of huge successes. Remember that little things count, too. Whatever makes you feel proud can go on your list.

There are four simple steps you can follow to keep an I-Did-It List and collect lots of proud feelings.

Hand out copies of "How to Keep an I-Did-It List." Read it to the students or ask them to read:

1. STOP everything and notice what's making you proud, then
2. FEEL the proud feeling, then
3. STORE it inside of you, then
4. WRITE it down as soon as you can.

Say:

Your list could include things like this:

- I took out the garbage without being told.

- I fed the cat.

- I studied for my math test.

- I remembered to ask about make-up work.

- I said hi to the new kid in school.

- I helped my little sister clean her room.

- I tried out for the softball team.

- I joined the math club.

End the activity by saying:

> Keeping an I-Did-It List helps you stick up for yourself—with yourself. It helps you gain personal power and build positive self-esteem from inside.

> Being proud of yourself doesn't mean being stuck-up, conceited, or feeling that you're better than other people. It just means enjoying your own accomplishments, skills, and abilities.

> Think of your I-Did-It List as a self-esteem savings account. It reminds you of how valuable and worthwhile you are.

> For the rest of the course, keep an I-Did-It List every day. And don't stop keeping your Happiness List. You'll find that it doesn't take much time to keep both lists—and it's worth it.

7. CLOSING

Summarize by saying:

> In this session, you learned that naming and claiming your dreams is an important part of getting to know yourself.

> You learned that you need to have two kinds of dreams: *near-future* dreams and *far-future* dreams. Your near-future dreams can help your far-future dreams come true.

> You practiced talking things over with yourself as a way to figure out how to claim your dreams and identify ways to make your dreams come true.

> You also learned about the I-Did-It List, a self-esteem savings account.

Say:

> **Before the next session, read pages 49 through 60 in *Stick Up for Yourself!* You've already read pages 57 through 60, but please look at them again.**
>
> **These pages are listed on the "Session Topics and Reading Assignments" handout you received at the beginning of the course. If anyone needs an extra copy, let me know.**
>
> **The next time we meet, we'll be talking about what it means to name and claim your needs.**

If necessary, tell students where and when the next session will be.

TALK THINGS OVER WITH YOURSELF
(TALK ABOUT DREAMS)

Ask yourself, "What are my future dreams?" Then name a dream for the near future or far future. Next, talk it over with yourself. Your talk might go like this:

SAY:

I want to _____ someday.

ASK:

What do I have to learn to make this dream happen?

SAY:

I can start by _____

_____

_____

ASK:

What else can I do?

SAY:

I can _____

_____

_____

HOW TO KEEP AN I–DID–IT LIST

Whenever something happens that makes you feel proud:

1. **STOP** everything and notice what's making you proud, then

2. **FEEL** the proud feeling, then

3. **STORE** it inside of you, then

4. **WRITE** it down as soon as you can.

Try to do this five times every day. Weekdays and weekends. School days and holidays. Be proud of yourself five times every day.

SESSION SEVEN
NAMING AND CLAIMING YOUR NEEDS

OVERVIEW...

Stick Up for Yourself!
Reading Assignment
pages 49–60

In this session, students learn to name and claim their needs. Seven basic needs are presented: relationships with other people; touching and holding; belonging and feeling "one" with others; being different and separate from others; nurturing other people; feeling worthwhile, valued, and admired; and having power in our relationships and our lives.

Students learn that the more they know about their needs, the more they can understand them and tell other people about them. Knowing their needs and thinking of ways to get them met are important ways to stick up for themselves. Students learn that their needs guide their decisions and help them define the kinds of people they are or want to become. They learn how their needs play a role in choosing and building relationships.

LEARNER OUTCOMES...

The purpose of this session is to help students:

- understand that part of sticking up for yourself is naming and claiming needs

- identify seven needs that are common to all people

- understand how talking things over with themselves can help them learn more about their needs

MATERIALS..

- copies of the student book, *Stick Up for Yourself!* [activities 2, 5]

- copies of the "Seven Needs" handout (page 84) [activity 3]

- materials for creating a mural [activity 4]

Tape to a wall before the session begins:

- a large oblong piece of white paper or posterboard with "Picture Your Need" written across the top

Put on a large table near the paper/posterboard:

- old magazines, catalogs, newspapers with pictures
- drawing paper, colored construction paper
- crayons, colored markers, colored pencils
- scissors, tape, glue
- copies of the "Talk Things Over with Yourself (Talk About Needs)" handout (page 85) [activity 5]

AGENDA . . . .

1. Introduce the session.
2. Review the reading assignment.
3. Lead the discussion "What Do You Need?"
4. Lead the art activity "Picture Your Need" to help students learn to identify how their needs relate to what they do in their daily lives.
5. Lead the activity "Talking Things Over with Yourself" to help students learn to identify their needs by having a conversation with themselves.
6. Review the reasons for keeping an I-Did-It List.
7. Close the session and assign the reading for Session 8.

ACTIVITIES . . . .

1. INTRODUCTION

Say:

> In this session, we'll talk about naming and claiming your needs, which is a way to get to know yourself. It's also a way to build personal power.
>
> All human beings have the same basic needs. When our needs are met, we're healthier, happier people.
>
> Sometimes it's difficult to get certain needs met right now. In this session, we'll learn what we might be able to do, even when we can't get our needs met.

2. READING

Ask students to quickly review pages 49–60 in *Stick Up for Yourself!* Tell them to raise their hands when they're done but to keep their books open. Then ask:

> **What do we sometimes really mean when we say we *need* something? Like "I need a new computer game" or "I need a haircut"?** *(It really means that we* want *something.)*
>
> **Is needing other people a sign we are strong or a sign we are weak? Find a sentence or two in your book that supports your answer.**

Have a volunteer read aloud these sentences from page 50 of the student book:

> If you need other people, if you have relationships with other people, then you aren't weak. *You're strong.* Needing is a source of strength.

> **Why is it sometimes hard for people to get enough touching and holding in our society? Find that part in your book and listen while I read it.**

Read aloud the following paragraph from page 51:

> Unfortunately, we live in a culture that confuses touching and holding with sex. That's why, as you get older, you may get mixed messages about touching and holding. Friends who touch each other are teased. Parents decide that their kids are too grown-up to be hugged and kissed. This is a problem with our culture; it isn't a problem with you. It's still okay to need touching and holding—now and for the rest of your life.

Remind them that they need to be very clear about the difference between *good touch* and *bad touch*. Say:

> *Good touch* **feels good and right. Your mom hugs you. Or your friends pat you on the back when you score a basket. Or your dad holds you and comforts you when you're feeling sad.**

> *Bad touch* **is when someone—usually a grown-up or an older child—touches you in a way that feels bad or wrong, or in a way you don't want. If that ever happens to you, it's *very* important to say NO! and get away as fast as you can. Then tell an adult you trust. You can also talk to an adult if you're ever confused about good and bad touch.**

Earlier in this course, in the session about claiming your feelings *(Session 5)*, you wrote in your notebook the names of adults you trust and can talk to about strong feelings. You can also talk to them about good touch and bad touch.

Ask:

Can anyone tell me what it means to feel "one" with other people? *(We feel we have things in common with them; we feel close to them; we care about them and they care about us; we learn from them and they learn from us.)*

Why do you think we need to belong and feel "one" with other people? *(This helps us know we're not alone.)*

Say:

At the same time we need to belong, we also need to be different and separate. We need to be ourselves. We go back and forth between these two needs.

We also need to nurture other people. It makes them feel good, and it makes us feel good inside.

Ask:

Can anyone tell me a time when someone nurtured you, or when you nurtured someone else?

Say:

We all need to feel worthwhile, valued, and admired. If other people aren't helping us feel worthwhile, valued, and admired, who can do that for us? *(We can affirm and encourage ourselves.)*

We need to feel we have power in our relationships and in our lives. We'll talk more about this need in the next session.

3. WHAT DO YOU NEED?

Hand out copies of "Seven Needs." Read it to the students, or ask volunteers to read each sentence in turn:

1. the need for relationships with other people
2. the need for touching and holding
3. the need to belong and feel "one" with others
4. the need to be different and separate
5. the need to nurture (to care for and help other people)
6. the need to feel worthwhile, valued, and admired
7. the need for power in our relationships and our lives

Ask:

> **If you need something, but you don't know what it is, how can you figure out what you need?** *(If someone suggests talking it over with yourself, agree and say you'll be practicing that later in the session.)*

> **Do you think our feelings or dreams might give us clues about our needs?**

Say:

> **If I'm feeling lonely, what need might I have?** *(The need for relationships with other people; the need for touching and holding; the need to belong and feel "one" with others.)*

> **If you dream of being in charge of your life and making all of your decisions without getting permission from anyone else, what need might this be?** *(The need for power in our relationships and our lives.)*

Ask the students to come up with other feelings or dreams and relate them to needs. If they have trouble doing this, you might offer one or more examples:

- I don't like hanging out with my friends right now. I want to spend more time on my own. What might I need? *(To be different and separate.)*

- I'm having trouble seeing that anything I do really matters. What might I need? *(To feel worthwhile, valued, and admired.)*

- I wish I were little again so I could curl up in my dad's lap and listen to a story. What might I need? *(To be touched and held.)*

End the activity by saying:

> **So far, we have practiced naming our needs. We have learned that our feelings and dreams can give us clues about our needs.**

4. PICTURE YOUR NEED

Call students' attention to the large piece of white paper or poster-board with "Picture Your Need" written across the top. Then say:

> **We're going to make a mural about needs.**

> **Each of you will find or draw a picture that relates to one of the seven basic needs. You'll find magazines and art supplies on the table.**

When you have your picture, tape or glue it to the mural. Don't tell anyone which need it relates to. Keep that a secret for now.

You might bring along your "Seven Needs" sheet to remind you of what the needs are.

When you've put your picture on the mural, return to your seat.

Remember, your picture should relate to one of the seven basic needs.

You'll have ten minutes to work on the mural, so let's get started.

Stop this part of the activity after ten minutes, even if some students are still working. When all students are back in their seats, say:

We're going to take a few minutes to see if we can guess the need that each of these pictures is about.

Point to each picture in turn and ask volunteers to guess which need it relates to. After one or two guesses, ask the student who put the picture on the mural to raise his or her hand. Then ask that person, "What need did you have in mind?"

NOTE: Take only about half a minute or so for each. Stop this part of the activity after five minutes.

End the activity by saying:

We're getting practice thinking about the basic needs and how they relate to our lives. Everyone has the same seven needs. It's important to know about them so we can try to get our needs met.

5. TALKING THINGS OVER WITH YOURSELF

Say:

You can learn a lot about your needs by talking things over with yourself. Today we're going to practice doing that.

Hand out copies of "Talk Things Over with Yourself (Talk About Needs)." Then say:

Before you work on your own, let's look over the script on page 60 in *Stick Up for Yourself!* to get some ideas of how to do this.

Notice that your "Talk Things Over with Yourself" sheet has questions like the script in the book, but there are blanks for you to fill in.

Take a few minutes and write about a need you have right now. You won't have to share your writing with anyone else unless you want to. This is just for you.

After a few moments, ask:

What did you learn from doing this?

Did anyone have trouble figuring out how to help yourself meet your need? By talking things over with yourself, you may get some ideas.

Does anyone want to share your need and tell us one thing you decided to do about it?

Allow time for students who want to share. Then end the activity by saying:

Keep this script in your notebook to help you remember the questions to ask when you want to talk needs over with yourself.

6. THE I-DID-IT LIST (REVIEW)

Say:

In the last session, you learned about the I-Did-It List, and I asked you to start keeping the list every day, just like you do the Happiness List.

How is it going? Are you finding things to put on your list—things you feel satisfied with and good about? Are you able to be proud of yourself five times every day?

Did anyone get stuck trying to make your list? Were you trying to find huge successes to write about? Remember that little things count, too. Whatever makes you feel proud can go on your list.

It may take a while for you to notice your successes. We sometimes train ourselves to notice the things we *don't* do well. That gets in the way of noticing our successes.

Just keep writing each day. Make it a habit, and soon it will get easier.

Remember that your I-Did-It List is like a self-esteem savings account. Don't let it be empty. It reminds you how valuable and worthwhile you are. And that's one of the seven basic needs!

7. CLOSING

Summarize by saying:

> In this session, you learned that naming and claiming your needs is an important part of getting to know yourself.
>
> You learned that everyone has seven basic needs, and you learned what they are.
>
> You practiced talking needs over with yourself as a way to figure out how to get a need met.
>
> You also heard a reminder about how important it is to keep writing your I-Did-It List.

Say:

> Before the next session, read pages 72 through 86 in *Stick Up for Yourself!* (up to "How to Live Happily Ever After").
>
> The next time we meet, we'll be talking about what it means to get and use power in your relationships and in your life. We'll learn the difference between *personal power* and *role power*.

If necessary, tell students where and when the next session will be.

OPTIONAL: BEFORE THE NEXT SESSION

Session 8 includes an optional "Power Tune" activity. If you plan to do the activity, say:

> We'll also listen to some songs about personal power. If you know a song you think says something about personal power, please bring in a cassette or CD a day or two before the next session.
>
> Remember that personal power means being *secure and confident inside yourself.* It's about being responsible, making choices, and getting to know yourself. When you're looking for a song to bring in, remember what personal power really means.

Preview songs before the next session. Make sure the lyrics are compatible with your program's standards. For example, you'll want to avoid songs with lyrics that are sexist, racist, sexually graphic, or violent.

SEVEN NEEDS

1. the need for relationships with other people

2. the need for touching and holding

3. the need to belong and feel "one" with others

4. the need to be different and separate

5. the need to nurture (to care for and help other people)

6. the need to feel worthwhile, valued, and admired

7. the need for power in our relationships and our lives

TALK THINGS OVER WITH YOURSELF
(TALK ABOUT NEEDS)

Ask yourself, "Is there anything I need right now?" Try to name your need. Then talk it over with yourself. Your talk might go something like this:

SAY:

I need _____

ASK:

How can I start to get my need met?

SAY:

I can _____

_____

_____

ASK:

What if that doesn't work?

SAY:

I can _____

_____

_____

SESSION EIGHT
GETTING AND USING POWER

OVERVIEW . . . .

Stick Up for Yourself!
Reading Assignment
pages 72–86 (up to
"How to Live Happily
Ever After")

In this session, students learn the difference between role power and personal power. Role power is something they have because of what they do (their role). Personal power is something they have because of who they are. Personal power is the most important kind of power they will ever have. It means they can have power over their own lives, even if they never have much role power.

Through discussion, students learn to identify choices they have in situations where they feel powerless. Identifying choices is presented as a way they can realize they have power in their lives.

LEARNER OUTCOMES . . . .

The purpose of this session is to help students:

- understand the differences between role power and personal power
- understand that their feelings help them recognize whether people are using power in a positive or negative way
- understand that their feelings help them recognize whether they are using power over others in a positive or negative way
- understand that when they are given choices, they feel powerful instead of powerless
- identify choices they can give themselves

MATERIALS . . . .

- copies of the student book, *Stick Up for Yourself!* [activity 2]
- chalkboard or flip chart [activities 2, 3]
- student notebooks [activity 3]
- *Optional:* CD/cassette player [activity 3]

AGENDA . . . .

1. Introduce the session.

2. Review the reading assignment.

3. Lead the activity "Role Power" to help students identify people in their lives who have role power over them. *Optional:* Lead the activity "Power Tune."

4. Lead the activity "Balance of Power" to help students identify ways to develop equal power in a relationship. *Optional:* Expand this activity to broaden the discussions.

5. Review the Happiness List and the I-Did-It List.

6. Close the session and assign the reading for Session 9.

ACTIVITIES . . . .

1. INTRODUCTION

Say:

You may remember that personal power has four parts. We've already talked about three of those parts: being responsible for your feelings and behavior, making choices, and getting to know yourself. In this session, we're going to talk about the fourth part: getting and using power in your relationships and your life.

This session will help you identify ways you already have power in your life, as well as new ways to use your personal power.

2. READING

Ask students to read or review pages 72–86 in *Stick Up for Yourself!* Tell them to raise their hands when they're done but to keep their books open. Then ask:

What are the two kinds of power? (*Personal power and role power.*)

As you ask the following questions, record the students' answers on a chalkboard or flip chart.

Who can tell me one difference between role power and personal power? What's another difference? Are there any more differences? Any more?

Students should mention the four differences described on pages 73–74:

> • Role power is something you have just because you're in a certain role. Personal power is something you get because you want it and you work for it.
>
> • Role power depends on having someone else to be powerful over. (A president without people to govern doesn't have much role power.) Personal power depends only on you.
>
> • Role power is something you might have to wait for. You might never have very much role power. Personal power is something you can have *right now*, if you want it. And you can have as much as you want.
>
> • Only some people can have role power. Anyone can have personal power. *You* can have personal power. *Even if many people have role power over you.*

Ask:

> **Why is it a big waste of energy to fight back against people who have role power over you?** *(It probably won't do any good; it might get you in trouble. You have to accept that there will always be people with role power over you.)*
>
> **What can you do with your energy instead of fighting back?**

End the activity by saying:

> **In this reading, you learned there are two kinds of power. Personal power is the most important kind of power you'll ever have. It means you can have power over your life, even if you never have much role power.**

3. ROLE POWER

Say:

> **Role power is power you have not because of *who you are*, but just because of *what you do*—in other words, your *role*.**
>
> **Right now, there are people in our lives who have role power over us. This is true for all of us.**

Talk briefly about people who have role power over you—and why they have role power. Then say:

> **Turn to a clean page in your notebook. Divide it into two columns by drawing a line down the center.** *(Show them how on the chalkboard or flip chart.)*

> **Write "Role power over me" at the top of the column on the left, and "How I feel about it" at the top of the column on the right.** *(Show them how.)*

Role power over me	How I feel about it

> **In the left column, list the people who have role power over you right now in your daily life. You can write the person's name or the person's role—like parent, math teacher, coach, and so on.**

> **In the right column, write a word or two that describes how you feel about that person's role power over you. You won't have to share your feelings unless you want to.**

You might suggest some words students could use: Okay, So-So, Crummy, No Problem, Super. Or they could use plus or minus symbols, or happy/neutral/sad faces. (You might draw these on the chalkboard or flip chart. A happy face has a smile; a neutral face has a straight-line mouth; a sad face has a frown.)

Give students a few minutes to work on their lists. Then ask:

> **Do you feel the same about all the people who have role power over you?**

> **Why do you think it feels okay when some people use role power over you, and not okay when others do?** *(You want students to discover that it depends partly on what they ask you to do and how they treat you.)*

Say:

> Choose one person on your list. Think about these questions: If you could switch roles and have role power over that person, what would you do the same as he or she does? What would you do differently?
>
> Who would like to share your thoughts?
>
> If you picture yourself in that person's role, does it make a difference? Is it easier to accept that he or she has role power over you?

End the activity by saying:

> When you accept that some people have role power over you, you can use your energy to build more personal power.

OPTIONAL: POWER TUNE

Depending on how much time is available, play one or more songs. After each song, ask:

> What words in the song do you remember?
>
> What do you think this song says about personal power?

End the activity by saying:

> There are many ways our culture talks about power. Songs are one way. Art is another way. Advertising is another way. Start noticing power images. When you see or hear one, think about whether it's about personal power or role power.

4. BALANCE OF POWER

NOTE: Talking about power in relationships can raise surprising or threatening feelings—including feelings about how students perceive their teachers (like you) using role power over them. Be aware of your own feelings, and take time later to be sure you have paid enough attention to what you were experiencing. See "Getting Support for Yourself" (page 7).

Ask:

> If you wanted to give a friend power over you, how would you do it? *(Possible answers: always do what they want to do, always say what they want to hear.)*

Say:

> **Sometimes we give friends power over us, and we don't even know we're doing it. Our feelings can help us be aware of times when we're giving away our power, or times when we're using power over other people.**
>
> **We're going to divide into five small groups. In your group, you'll be talking about a time when you felt you *didn't* have equal power with someone else. It may even be a time when you felt totally powerless.**

After dividing the class into small groups, point to each group and say:

> **Group 1, you'll be talking about situations with a *friend*.**
>
> **Group 2, you'll be talking about situations with your *peer group*.**
>
> **Group 3, you'll be talking about situations with a *sibling*—a brother or sister. (*Make sure all members of this group have siblings. If they don't, exchange members with another group.*)**
>
> **Group 4, you'll be talking about situations with a *teacher*.**
>
> **Group 5, you'll be talking about situations with a *parent*.**

Say:

> **Each of you will give one example of a situation where you *don't* feel you have equal power, or you feel powerless. Tell the group how you feel when you don't have power. Then ask them for ideas about how you could get more power or equal power. They should come up with as many realistic choices as they can.**

Write on the chalkboard or flip chart:

1. Give example
2. Say how you feel
3. Ask for ideas
4. Listen

> **Keep it moving so everyone in your group has a chance to give an example and get ideas for choices.**

After a few minutes, bring the groups back together. Say:

> **I need one volunteer from Group 1 to describe a situation that was discussed and tell what the group suggested.**

When the volunteer has finished, ask the class:

How many of you have been in this kind of situation?

Does anyone have any other ideas to offer—ways that person could get more power or equal power?

Continue until you have heard at least one person from each group.

NOTE: Since the reading assignment for this session includes a section on "How to Deal with Bullies," it's possible that one or more groups might describe a bullying situation. If this happens, make time for a brief discussion about bullying. You might review the facts about bullying on pages 82–83 of the student book, and the suggestions on page 84.

End the activity by saying:

In this activity, we talked about ways to overcome feeling powerless, and ways to develop equal power. It's important to focus on what *we* have power over and choices *we* can make, instead of trying to change other people.

OPTIONAL: POWER TALKS

Instead of having each group talk about power in only one context—i.e., with a friend, sibling, or peer group—you may want to schedule another session or sessions so each group can talk about power in all contexts. This would give students a greater opportunity to explore ways to develop equal power in all of their relationships.

5. THE HAPPINESS LIST AND I-DID-IT LIST (REVIEW)

Ask:

How are you doing with your Happiness List and I-Did-It List?

Share some of the positive things you've been noticing since you began keeping your own lists.

Are you finding things to put on your Happiness List—things that made you smile? Is it getting to be a habit to notice things that make you happy?

Is it getting easier to identify five things you did each day that you feel proud of?

Remind students of the four steps for keeping each list:

1. STOP everything and notice what's making you happy or proud, then
2. FEEL the happy or proud feeling, then
3. STORE it inside of you, then
4. WRITE it down as soon as you can.

Say:

> The important thing is to keep writing your lists every day, and soon it will be a habit.
>
> The Happiness List is your collection of good and happy feelings. Don't stop collecting.
>
> Your I-Did-It List reminds you how valuable and worthwhile you are. When your self-esteem is strong, you'll feel your personal power.

6. CLOSING

Summarize by saying:

> In this session, you learned that there are two kinds of power: *personal power* and *role power.*
>
> You talked with each other about ways to develop more power or equal power in your relationship.
>
> You learned that having choices gives you more personal power.

Say:

> Before the next session, read pages 91 through 97 in *Stick Up for Yourself!* (up to "Keep an I-Did-It List"). Also read pages 101 through 110.
>
> The next time we meet, we'll be talking about ways to build your self-esteem.

If necessary, tell students where and when the next session will be.

SESSION NINE
BUILDING SELF—ESTEEM

OVERVIEW . . . .

Stick Up for Yourself!
Reading Assignment
pages 91–97 (up to
"Keep an I-Did-It
List") and 101–110

In this session, students learn what self-esteem really means and practice ways to build positive self-esteem. They begin to understand and identify how their inner voices (what they are thinking, feeling, or imagining about themselves) influence their self-esteem. They learn that sometimes their inner voices have a powerful impact on how they feel about themselves. They learn to become more aware of those inner voices and practice ways to change them, so the judgments they are continuously giving themselves about themselves are positive and self-affirming. Students also think about things they can begin doing every day to be good to themselves and take care of themselves.

LEARNER OUTCOMES . . . .

The purpose of this session is to help students:

- understand that they need positive self-esteem in order to stick up for themselves
- identify good things about themselves
- understand what self-esteem really means
- understand how to change critical, blaming, and comparing inner voices into self-affirming inner voices
- identify good things to begin doing for themselves

MATERIALS . . . .

- copies of the student book, *Stick Up for Yourself!* [activities 2, 3]
- student notebooks [activities 2,3]
- slips of paper and a sack to put them in [activity 4]
- chalkboard or flip chart [activity 4]

- copies of the "Six Good Things to Do for Yourself" handout (page 104) [activity 5]
- sheets of paper [activity 6]

AGENDA ....

1. Introduce the session.

2. Review the reading assignment.

3. Introduce the self-esteem quiz on pages 92–95 in *Stick Up for Yourself!* and have students take the quiz.

4. Lead the activity "Time to Talk Back" to help students learn to change negative, critical inner voices into self-affirming inner voices.

5. Assign the activity "Six Good Things to Do for Yourself" as homework for the next session.

6. Have students write role-play scenarios to be used in the final session.

7. Close the session. (There is no reading assignment for Session 10.)

ACTIVITIES ....

1. INTRODUCTION

Say:

In this session, we'll focus on positive self-esteem. In order to stick up for yourself, you need to feel good about yourself—to feel valuable and worthwhile.

We'll practice some tools that will help you build positive self-esteem.

2. READING

Ask a volunteer to read aloud page 91 of *Stick Up for Yourself!* Then say:

Turn to a clean page in your notebook. Quickly write five good things about yourself that you would tell Mr. Morse.

Allow a moment or two for students to do the writing. Then ask:

Who would like to share one or two things you wrote?

Comment positively on what students say about themselves. ("I'm glad to know that," "I didn't know that about you," "That's terrific," "That's something to be proud of.")

Say:

> If you've been keeping your I-Did-It List, you all know lots more than five good things about yourselves. Your self-esteem savings account is growing every day.

> Before we start learning more ways to build self-esteem, there's something important you need to know.

Read aloud the following from page 95 of the student book:

> You might have heard people talk about self-esteem as if it's a bad thing. They think self-esteem means bragging, being stuck-up, and believing you're better than everyone else.
>
> They're mistaken.
>
> Self-esteem means being proud of yourself and feeling that pride on the inside. Not because you've told yourself, "I'm special and wonderful." Not because other people have said, "You're special and wonderful." Words don't create pride. Actions create pride. *Self-esteem means being proud of yourself because you've done things you're proud of.*

Say:

> No one can *give* you self-esteem. No one can take it away. It's not about anyone else. It's just about *you*.

3. LISTENING TO YOUR INNER VOICES

Say:

> We're going to take a few minutes to do the self-esteem quiz in your book.

> Turn to a clean page in your notebook. Number down the left side from one to ten.

> There are ten questions, and I'll read them aloud. Each question describes a different situation. You choose the answer—a or b— that sounds *most like* the way you think or talk to yourself in that kind of situation.

Of course, the answers won't be *exactly* what you'd say. Don't worry about that. Focus on how the answers *feel*. Which one feels most like you, a or b? Write the answer letter in your notebook.

Don't answer the way you think you *should* answer. Answer the way you really *would* answer. You won't have to share your answers. No one will know them but you. The point of this quiz is to learn something about yourself.

Read the questions and answers:

1. When you get up in the morning and look at yourself in the mirror, what do you say?
(a) "I look great this morning! And I'm going to have a great day."
(b) "Oh, no, not me again! I'm so ugly! Why did I bother to get out of bed?"

2. When you fail at something or make a mistake, what do you tell yourself?
(a) "Everyone has the right to fail or make mistakes every day. Including me."
(b) "I blew it again! I can't do anything right! I should have known better."

3. When you achieve something, what do you say to yourself?
(a) "I'm proud of myself."
(b) "I could have done even better if I had tried harder. It wasn't good enough."

4. You've just talked with someone who has role power over you. (Like a parent, a teacher, or a coach.) What do you tell yourself?
(a) "I handled that pretty well."
(b) "I can't believe I acted so stupid! I always say dumb things."

5. You've just left the first meeting of a new club you joined. What do you say to yourself?
(a) "That was fun. I met some people I liked. They even laughed at the joke I told."
(b) "I talked too much, and nobody liked me. Everyone hated my joke."

6. You've just left a friend's house after playing together. What do you tell yourself?
(a) "That was fun. We really like each other!"
(b) "My friend was just pretending to like me. I probably won't get invited back ever again."

7. When someone gives you a compliment, what do you say to yourself?
(a) "That's nice, and it makes me feel good. Besides, I deserve it!"
(b) "Nobody gives you a compliment unless they want something back. Besides, I don't deserve it."

8. When someone you care about lets you down, what do you tell yourself?
(a) "My feelings are hurt, but I'll get over it. Later, I can try to find out what happened."
(b) "This proves that person doesn't care about me."

9. When you let down someone you care about, what do you say to yourself?
(a) "It isn't nice, and it isn't fun, but sometimes people let each other down. I'll admit what I did, say I'm sorry, hope the person will forgive me, and get on with my life."
(b) "How could I do such a terrible thing? I'm so ashamed. No wonder nobody likes me."

10. When you feel needy or unsure of yourself, what do you tell yourself?
(a) "Everyone feels this way sometimes. I'll ask my dad for a hug or curl up with my Teddy bear, and I'll feel better soon."
(b) "Why can't I grow up and stop being a baby? What's wrong with me?"

Say:

Now count your a answers and multiply by ten.

Count your b answers and multiply by five.

Add the two scores together. Look at the key on page 95 of your book to find out what your score suggests about your self-esteem.

You don't need to share your score with anyone. It's for your own information.

Ask:

How many of you agree with your self-esteem rating?

Say:

If your score is low, don't worry about it. You're already practicing one important way to build your self-esteem—the I-Did-It List. You'll learn more ways today.

Before we leave the quiz and go on to something else, let's look at some of the answers one more time.

If your book isn't already open to page 92, where the quiz starts, please open it now.

Sometimes we blame or criticize ourselves. If we do this a lot, it lowers our self-esteem. Some of the answers in the quiz are examples of how we might blame or criticize ourselves.

Read the answers until you find an example of blaming. What did you find?

Now find an example of criticizing. What is it?

Can you find another blaming or criticizing answer?

If students have trouble with this, suggest that they read the b answers. Then say:

Think for a minute about yourself. Do you blame or criticize yourself? A little bit? A lot? Now and then? You don't need to tell us your answer. Just think about it.

Sometimes we compare ourselves with other people. When we do, we often end up feeling that we don't measure up—that other people are smarter, or better looking, or they run faster, or they have more friends.

If we spend a lot of time comparing, we may decide we aren't valuable or worthwhile unless we're better than someone else.

Can you find an answer in the quiz that's an example of comparing?

If students can't find one, suggest that they look at b in question 5.

Ask:

Do you ever compare yourself with other people? Do you do it a lot? Again, just think about it; you don't have to answer out loud.

End the activity by saying:

> *Blaming, criticizing,* and *comparing* are three shaming inner voices we sometimes hear. Those voices hurt our self-esteem.
>
> But we don't have to listen. We can talk back!

4. TIME TO TALK BACK

Ask:

> What do you think an "inner voice" is? *(You want them to say that it's the way we talk to ourselves—including the things we tell ourselves about ourselves. It's how we treat ourselves, how we behave toward ourselves in ways that produce positive or negative feelings.)*

Say:

> If your inner voice is blaming, criticizing, or comparing, you can change it. There are three ways to do this.

Write on the chalkboard or flip chart:

> By having new words to say to yourself.
> By having new feelings of love and respect for yourself.
> By imagining a new inner voice that's like the voice of someone who cares about you and encourages you.

Ask:

> Can you think of one thing you sometimes tell yourself that's blaming or criticizing?

Hand out the slips of paper. Say:

> Write one thing you say to yourself when you're being hard on yourself. You don't have to sign your name. When you're done, come up and put your slip of paper in the sack.

Take a few moments to silently read through the slips. Then say:

> We tell ourselves a lot of shaming things, don't we? I do it, too. One thing I catch myself saying is, "_____, you are so _____." *(Fill in the blanks with your name and something you say to yourself— impatient, stubborn, forgetful, clumsy, etc.)*

Say:

> I'm going to write five of the things you mentioned on the board. Don't worry; no one will know who wrote what.

Write five student comments on the chalkboard or flip chart. Then say:

> **We can train ourselves to change those shaming inner voices. Let's practice.**
>
> **First, let's think about new words to say. If you say something like this** *(point to a student comment)* **to yourself, what new words could you say instead?**

Guide students to come up with positive alternatives to all five of the shaming comments. (You might need to give an example or two to get them started.) Then say:

> **Next, let's think about new feelings. What have you been doing in this course that might help you remember happy or proud feelings and memories?** *(Keeping a Happiness List and an I-Did-It List.)*
>
> **These feelings and memories can help you change your inner voices. Instead of "You're so _____," you can tell yourself, "Remember when you _____?"**

Fill in the first blank with one of the student comments from the chalkboard or flip chart. Fill in the second blank with a positive comment related to the student comment; you'll have to make this up, since you won't know what students are writing in their Happiness List and I-Did-It List. For examples, see page 101 of the student book.

Say:

> **Finally, let's try to imagine new inner voices that are like the voices of people who care about us and encourage us.**
>
> **Think of someone who cares about you. Someone who likes you, admires you, respects you, and helps you. Imagine the sound of that person's voice. If that person heard you say _____** *(fill in with one of the student comments)*, **what might he or she say instead?**
>
> **Say those words to yourself. Imagine the other person saying them. Hear the person's voice inside your head.**
>
> **Would anyone like to tell us who you're thinking about right now? Whose voice are you hearing?**

End the activity by saying:

The next time you hear a shaming inner voice, try to remember the three things that can help you change it to a positive, affirming inner voice: New words. New feelings. The comforting, encouraging voice of someone who cares about you.

These three things will help you build positive self-esteem.

5. SIX GOOD THINGS TO DO FOR YOURSELF

Hand out copies of "Six Good Things to Do for Yourself." Then say:

This is your homework assignment.

When you get home, read the six good things at the top of this sheet. Then fill in the blanks at the bottom.

Do as many of these good things as you can before the next session. Bring your sheet to the session. We'll talk about it then.

If you need ideas, look at pages 106 and 107 of *Stick Up for Yourself!*

6. WRITING A ROLE-PLAY SCENARIO

Hand out the sheets of paper. Say:

In this course, we've been learning new ways to stick up for ourselves. Next week, in our last session, you're going to role-play ways to stick up for yourselves, using your own role-play ideas.

Write about something that's happening in your life—a situation where you'd like to stick up for yourself. Don't sign your name. Just describe the situation.

If students have trouble thinking of something to write, give a few examples:

- A kid at school teases you all the time.

- Your sister steals the remote when you're watching TV.

- Your parents make you go to bed at 9:00 every night. You think that's too early.

- Your soccer coach yells at you—especially if you make a mistake. He screams at you in front of the whole team.

Give students time to write, then collect their papers.

End the activity by saying:

Next week, we'll role-play as many of these as we have time for. This will give us new ideas about how to stick up for ourselves.

NOTE: If you don't have time for this writing activity but you still want to do the role-playing in Session 9, you can use the ideas on the "Role-Playing Scenarios" handout (page 113).

7. CLOSING

Summarize by saying:

In this session, you learned some ways to strengthen your self-esteem.

You took a quiz to find out how your self-esteem is right now, and you thought about whether you agree or disagree with the score. Either way, you know that your I-Did-It List can help you build positive self-esteem.

You thought of ways you blame, criticize, or compare yourself. You learned how to change a shaming inner voice into a positive, affirming inner voice. A positive inner voice is important to your self-esteem.

Say:

Before the next session, be sure to do your homework. Fill in the "Six Good Things to Do for Yourself" sheet, try some of your ideas—you can start today—and bring the sheet with you to the next session.

The next session is the last session for this course.

If necessary, tell students where and when the next session will be.

BEFORE THE NEXT SESSION

During the final session, you'll ask students to complete a course evaluation. (See "About the Evaluations" on pages 6–7.) You might use the form on page 114, or you might prefer to create your own evaluation. You'll need to decide in advance so you'll have copies available to hand out next time.

If you want to ask parents/caregivers to evaluate the course, you can use the form on page 115 or create your own. Have copies ready for the next session if you want to send them home with the students.

SIX GOOD THINGS TO DO FOR YOURSELF

1. Choose something to do just for fun. Then do it whenever you can.
2. Give yourself a treat every day. This can be almost anything, as long as it's just for you.
3. Forgive yourself for something you did in the past.
4. Do at least one thing every day that's good for your body.
5. Do at least one thing every day that's good for your brain.
6. Find adults you can trust and talk to. Let your feelings guide you to the right people. Pick three or more you feel safe with. Pick those who care enough to listen and try to understand how you feel.

MY PLAN

1. I'll do this just for fun

_____

2. I'll give myself this treat

_____

3. I'll forgive myself for

_____

4. I'll do this for my body

_____

5. I'll do this for my brain

_____

6. These are adults I can trust and talk to

_____

_____

_____

SESSION TEN
STICKING UP FOR YOURSELF FROM NOW ON

OVERVIEW . . . .

The final session reviews the ways students have been learning to stick up for themselves. Through role play, students are able to demonstrate their understanding of the various tools they can use to stick up for themselves.

LEARNER OUTCOMES . . . .

The purpose of this session is to help students:

- review the tools they learned to use in this course: the Happiness List, the I-Did-It List, and Talking Things Over with Yourself

- demonstrate through role play ways to stick up for themselves

- evaluate their progress toward their goals, which they described in writing in Session 1, activity 6

- evaluate the course as a whole

MATERIALS . . . .

- *Optional:* single copies of the "Talk Things Over with Yourself" scripts (pages 63, 74, and 85) for your reference [activity 4]

- student notebooks [activities 4, 7]

- students' completed "Six Good Things to Do for Yourself" home-work assignments from Session 9 (students should bring these) [activity 2]

- the scenarios students wrote in Session 9 (you collected these at the end of the session); a box or sack to put them in [activity 6]

- *Optional:* copies of the "Role-Playing Scenarios" handout (page 113) [activity 6]

- copies of the "Student's Course Evaluation" (page 114) or your own evaluation form [activity 8]
- *Optional:* copies of the "Parent's/Caregiver's Course Evaluation" (page 115) or your own evaluation form [activity 8]

AGENDA ....

1. Introduce the session.
2. Review the "Six Good Things to Do for Yourself" homework assignment from Session 9.
3. Lead the discussion "Our Lists—Another Look."
4. Lead the activity "Keep Talking Things Over with Yourself."
5. Lead the activity "One New Thing I Do to Stick Up for Myself."
6. Lead the role-play activity in which students help each other identify ways to stick up for themselves.
7. Ask students to do a self-evaluation of their progress in the course. They will read the goals that they wrote during Session 1 and decide whether they met their goals.
8. Ask students to evaluate the course as a whole.
9. Close the session.

ACTIVITIES ....

1. INTRODUCTION

Say:

> In this final session, we'll review some of the things we've learned in the course.

> We'll also do some role playing to help each other find new ways to stick up for ourselves.

2. SIX GOOD THINGS TO DO FOR YOURSELF

Say:

> In the last session, you had a homework assignment. Let's find out how that went.

> Take out your "Six Good Things to Do for Yourself" assignment sheets.

Ask:

> Who would like to tell us what you did just for fun?
>
> Which of you gave yourself a treat? Would you like to tell us what you gave yourself? Was it hard to think of a treat to give yourself every day? How might you make it simpler?
>
> Who wants to talk about forgiving yourself for something you did in the past? Was this hard to do? Why do you think it's important to forgive yourself?
>
> What did you do that was good for your body? Did anyone decide to eat differently? Get more sleep? Exercise?
>
> How did you take care of your brain? Did you find something new to read, or think about, or look at, or listen to each day?
>
> Maybe you found an adult to talk to—someone who could help you answer some questions, or who was willing to listen to something that was on your mind. Does anyone have anything to say about that?

End the activity by saying:

> Remember, one way to stick up for yourself is to take good care of yourself. The way we take care of ourselves one day might be different than what we do the next day. What counts is to keep at it. This is something that will be important throughout your entire life.

3. OUR LISTS—ANOTHER LOOK

Say:

> We can teach ourselves to notice things we do and feel proud of. What's one thing we learned to do that helps us notice and take credit for what we do each day? *(You want them to mention the I-Did-It List.)*
>
> Why is it important to collect good feelings? How can we do that? *(You want them to talk about the Happiness List.)*
>
> Don't forget, your lists are important. Keep adding to them. Your Happiness List is a great way to collect and store good feelings. Your I-Did-It List is a self-esteem savings account.

What if you have a feeling you want to collect, or you do something you're proud of, but you don't have a notebook with you to write it down? *(STOP everything and notice it; FEEL the happy/proud feeling; STORE it inside of you; WRITE it down as soon as you can.)*

Even if you don't carry a notebook around all the time, you could stick a piece of paper in your pocket to use for your lists.

Encourage students to find notebooks they can carry and use throughout the day. You may want to show them some small notebooks—maybe some you have used to keep your own lists. Or show them sheets of paper you've written on. Tell them there are many kinds of small notebooks they can easily carry in a pocket, purse, or backpack.

Say:

Plan your time so you can review your lists during the last few minutes before you go to bed at night. Feel the happy, proud feelings all over again.

Every so often, read through your lists and enjoy your good feelings again. Or pick something to experience again.

4. KEEP TALKING THINGS OVER WITH YOURSELF

NOTE: As you lead this activity, you may want to refer to the "Talk Things Over with Yourself" scripts on 63, 74, and 85. To avoid having to flip through the book, have copies of the scripts available.

Say:

What can we talk over with ourselves? *(Feelings, needs, and dreams.)*

Can anyone tell me how we can talk things over with ourselves? Let's start with feelings. How can we talk over a feeling with ourselves? How can we start? What question can we ask? *(How am I feeling today?)*

After you name the feeling, what can you ask? Find the script in your notebook, if you need help remembering. *(When you know the feeling, you ask, "Why am I feeling _____? What's happened that I feel _____ about?" Then ask what you can do about the feeling.)*

Follow this procedure to review the process of talking over needs and dreams with yourself.

End the activity by saying:

> **You can't always find someone else to talk to, even when you really need to talk. But you can always talk things over with yourself. This can help you understand your feelings, dreams, and needs, and give you ideas for what to do.**

5. ONE NEW THING I DO TO STICK UP FOR MYSELF

Say:

> **I'm going to go around the room. I'd like each of you to tell me one new thing you're doing to stick up for yourself *with other people*.**

Give each student a chance to contribute. Then say:

> **Now I'm going to go around the room again. I'd like each of you to tell me one new thing you're doing to stick up for yourself *with yourself*.**

If students have trouble with this, you might ask, "Are you doing anything differently when you make a mistake?"

Congratulate students for sticking up for themselves. Then say:

> **Keep noticing ways you're sticking up for yourself. Tell yourself you're doing a good job.**

> **You can learn a lot by watching how other people stick up for themselves. Let's do that next.**

6. ROLE PLAYS

Say:

> **In the last session, you each wrote about something that's happening in your life—a situation where you'd like to stick up for yourself.**

> **We're going to role-play some of those situations so we can learn from each other.**

Divide the class into pairs. Each pair will do at least one role play—or more, depending on the size of your class and how much time you have available.

Ask someone from each pair to come up and draw a piece of paper (role-playing scenario) from the box or sack.

NOTE: If you didn't have time in Session 9 for students to write scenarios, hand out copies of "Role-Playing Scenarios." Assign a scenario to each pair, or let students choose the ones they want to do.

When every pair has a scenario, say:

Read about the situation you will role-play, then decide who plays which role. You'll have a few minutes to rehearse.

After a few minutes, bring the class back together. Ask for volunteers to go first. Tell them to read the scenario out loud, then do the role play.

After the role play, ask the class:

What ideas did you get from this role play? Do you understand what you might do to stick up for yourself in this situation? What's clear? What isn't clear?

Allow a few moments for discussion. Then thank the first pair and ask for volunteers to go second.

Continue with this procedure—role play, then discuss—until all pairs have participated. Then ask the class:

Did you learn at least one new way to stick up for yourself? Where do you think you might try it?

End the activity by saying:

We are all role models for each other.

We can learn a lot from each other. We still have to make our own decisions because we're responsible for our own feelings and behavior. But it helps to get ideas from other people.

7. STUDENT SELF-EVALUATION

Say:

During the first session, you each set a goal for yourself for this course. You described it in writing in your notebook. Now I want you to find that page in your notebook.

You wrote an ending to this sentence:

> In this course, I want to learn new ways
> to stick up for myself when…

Take a few minutes and write, on the same page, any new ways you've learned to stick up for yourself. This is just for you; you don't need to share it with anyone else.

Ask:

How many of you think you met your goal?

Remind students that change takes time. Even if they aren't yet where they want to be, they're learning and growing. They haven't failed.

8. STUDENT'S COURSE EVALUATION

Hand out copies of the "Student's Course Evaluation" or your own evaluation form. Say:

I want to find out how you feel about this course as a whole. I'm going to give you a form to fill out. Please tell me what you want me to know about the course. It will help me when I teach the course to another group of students. If you need more room to write, you can use the back of the sheet.

Give students a few minutes to complete the evaluation. Be sure to collect the forms before students leave the room.

OPTIONAL: PARENT'S/CAREGIVER'S COURSE EVALUATION

If you want to ask parents/caregivers to evaluate the course, you can give students copies of the "Parent's/Caregiver's Course Evaluation" to take home with them. Or mail them separately.

9. SESSION CLOSING

Summarize by saying:

In this course, you learned new ways to strengthen your self-esteem and stick up for yourself. You have some tools you can use every day, and we reviewed those in this session—the Happiness List, the I-Did-It List, and Talking Things Over with Yourself.

Say:

Thank you for your part—sharing your feelings and thoughts, and helping each other learn new ways to stick up for yourselves. Remember, change takes time. Keep practicing the tools you've learned.

You can continue developing personal power and positive self-esteem for the rest of your life. Keep sticking up for yourself with others—and yourself.

ROLE-PLAYING SCENARIOS

1. You're at a movie and the person behind you is loud and annoying.

2. A teacher doesn't give you the full directions for an assignment, so you don't get a good grade.

3. Your parents blame you for something you didn't do.

4. Your parents break a promise they made to you.

5. A friend says that your entry in a contest was dumb.

6. Someone in your class always bugs you and calls you names.

7. Someone teases you about the boy (girl) you like.

8. You're with a group of your friends. They're planning to get even with someone who did something they didn't like. You tell your friends you want to stay out of it, and they get mad at you.

9. The teacher asks a question. You raise your hand, and nobody else does. The teacher won't call on you.

10. Your coach doesn't give your team any credit for trying.

STUDENT'S COURSE EVALUATION

1. I am keeping a Happiness List... *(circle one answer)*

   every day   most days   now and then   never

2. I am keeping an I-Did-it List...

   every day   most days   now and then   never

3. One way I learned to stick up for myself is... *(write your answer)*

   _____

   _____

4. I am talking *feelings* over with myself...

   every day   most days   now and then   never

5. I am talking *dreams* over with myself...

   every day   most days   now and then   never

6. I am talking *needs* over with myself ...

   every day   most days   now and then   never

7. I am more aware of my inner voices...

   every day   most days   now and then   never

8. The tool that helped me most in this course was...

   Happiness List   I-Did-It List   Talking Things Over with Myself

9. The thing I learned the most about in this course was...

   _____

10. I wish there had been more _____ in this course.

11. I wish there had been less _____ in this course.

12. Do you have any other comments or suggestions? Write them on the back of this sheet.

STICK UP FOR YOURSELF!
PARENT'S/CAREGIVER'S COURSE EVALUATION

1. Have you observed any changes in your child's behavior since he or she began taking this course? In particular, is there anything you have noticed that makes you think your child is developing new ways to stick up for himself or herself?

   If you feel comfortable doing so, please describe what you have observed.

   _____

   _____

   _____

2. Did your child bring home the book *Stick Up for Yourself! Every Kid's Guide to Personal Power and Positive Self-Esteem* and give you a chance to read it?   YES   NO

3. Did you read the book?   YES   NO

4. Did your child talk with you about what we were discussing in the course?

   Every day   Most days   Now and then   Never

5. Did your child tell you about the Happiness List and I-Did-It List we were keeping?

   YES   NO

6. Do you feel that this course was a good experience for your child? Why or why not?

   _____

   _____

   _____

7. When we teach the course again, what do you think we should tell parents about it?

   _____

   _____

   _____

8. Do you have any other comments or suggestions? If so, please write them on the back of this page.

Please return this form to _____

From *A Teacher's Guide to Stick Up for Yourself!* by Gershen Kaufman, Ph.D., Lev Raphael, Ph.D., and Pamela Espeland, copyright © 2000.
Free Spirit Publishing Inc., Minneapolis, MN; 866/703-7322; *www.freespirit.com.*
This page may be photocopied for individual, classroom, or small group work only.

ADDITIONAL ACTIVITIES ACROSS THE CURRICULUM

CURRICULUM-RELATED ACTIVITIES...................................

The activities in this section allow you to reinforce concepts students are learning in this course. They are related to curriculum areas.

LANGUAGE ARTS AND CREATIVE WRITING

1. In a novel or short story, ask students to find examples of ways the writer lets us know what the characters are feeling.

   Give these examples:

   He looked down at the ground as he walked. His hands were in his pockets.
   What might he be feeling? Why?

   She was practically skipping down the hall.
   What might she be feeling? Why?

   John looked at his test results and said, "Oh, yes!"
   What might John be feeling? Why?

2. Ask students to write a paragraph that describes a feeling, without naming the feeling.

SOCIAL STUDIES

1. Ask students to find pictures of people in newspapers and magazines. Ask them to identify what they think the people in the pictures might have been feeling.

2. Tell students that politicians know that one way to get public support is to get people's feelings involved in an issue. Ask them to watch the evening news and try to find an example in which a politician may have been trying to "trigger" a certain feeling. Ask them to tell what the politician said that made them think it was an attempt to get people to feel a certain way about the issue.

3. Find headlines in newspapers or magazines that use names of feelings or describe/convey feelings.

4. Have students do research to find out if people in various cultures express their feelings in the same ways.

ART

To help students learn how to draw nonverbal clues that show behavior, ask them how they would draw inanimate objects so they look like they have feelings. Divide them into groups, and ask them to come up with ideas. *Examples:* an angry pencil, a sad house, a depressed table, a furious lamp.

FILM AND TELEVISION

Show a film or video with the sound turned off. Have students watch the faces on the film or video, then try to name the feelings displayed. Use the list of feelings on page 25 of the student book. You might also include the combined feelings (contempt, jealousy, loneliness, down mood) described on pages 40–44.

MUSIC

Ask students to bring in cassettes and/or CDs with songs that always make them feel happy. Preview the songs, then use appropriate songs as background music during another group activity.

OTHER LANGUAGES

Have students translate the names of feelings into another language that they are studying or would like to study. Tell them to make a poster showing each word in English and in as many other languages as they can find.

SOCIAL ACTIVITIES . . . .

An important part of this course is the social interaction among students. During the course, you may want to arrange social activities that extend beyond the regular session time. This section gives you some ideas.

BREAKS

During breaks, encourage students to get to know someone they don't already know.

Tell the students you will have a "Spotlight Minute" after the break. This can be a signal that anyone in the group can tell something interesting they learned about someone else during the break.

PHONE CALLS

When students are making new friends, they sometimes find it scary to make phone calls to each other. Have each student exchange phone numbers with one other person. During the week, they should call each other to say "Hello!" and "How's it going?" Have them decide who will call first. Ask them to think about what they might talk about. Ask them why they sometimes feel nervous about making a phone call. *Examples:* They might think the other person won't be glad to hear from them, or they might be afraid someone else will answer the phone.

PARTIES

Plan a party for the end of the course. Ask volunteers to help plan it. Ask the volunteers to make up a recipe for the party which tells each class member what to bring to the party. *Example:* 1 joke, 1 board game, a small can of pop, 2 snacks to share.

RESOURCES

Albert, Linda. *Cooperative Discipline.* Circle Pines, MN: American Guidance Service, 1996. Ways to foster cooperation, personal responsibility, and a sense of belonging in the classroom—and allow students to maintain their dignity when classroom problems arise.

Alberti, Robert E., and Michael L. Emmons. *Your Perfect Right: A Guide to Assertive Living.* Seventh edition. Atascadero, CA: Impact Publishers, 1995. The revised and updated edition of a classic guide to equal-relationship assertiveness includes step-by-step procedures, detailed examples, and exercises.

Benson, Peter, Judy Galbraith, and Pamela Espeland. *What Kids Need to Succeed: Proven, Practical Ways to Raise Good Kids.* Identifies 40 developmental assets (including personal power and self-esteem) that all kids need to lead healthy, productive, positive lives, then gives more than 500 concrete suggestions for building assets at home, at school, in the community, and in the congregation.

Bloch, Douglas. *Positive Self-Talk for Children: Teaching Self-Esteem Through Affirmations.* New York: Bantam Doubleday Dell, 1993. A step-by-step guide to helping children build self-esteem, a sense of independence, and greater optimism. Provides affirmations for every stage in a child's development and features chapters that help adults deal with their own negative tendencies.

Canfield, Jack, and Harold Clive Wells. *100 Ways to Enhance Self-Concept in the Classroom: A Handbook for Teachers, Counselors, and Group Leaders.* Second edition. Needham Heights, MA: Allyn & Bacon, 1994. Over 100 fun exercises enhance students' self-concept and self-esteem. This perennial best-seller helps teachers build a validating, searching, positive, and success-oriented community in any classroom.

Espeland, Pamela, and Rosemary Wallner. *Making the Most of Today: Daily Readings for Young People on Self-Awareness, Creativity, and Self-Esteem.* Minneapolis, MN: Free Spirit Publishing, 1998. Daily readings guide young people through a whole year of positive thinking and practical lifeskills.

Espeland, Pamela, and Elizabeth Verdick. *Making Every Day Count: Daily Readings for Young People on Solving Problems, Setting Goals, and Feeling Good About Yourself.* Minneapolis, MN: Free Spirit Publishing, 1998. A year's worth of daily inspiration, affirmation, and advice helps kids face challenges, plan for the future, and appreciate their unique and wonderful qualities.

Glennon, Will. *200 Ways to Raise a Girl's Self-Esteem: An Indispensable Guide for Parents, Teachers and Other Concerned Caregivers.* Berkeley, CA: Conari Press, 1999. A wealth of practical advice for helping girls boost their confidence, strengthen their self-image, and hold their own in the world.

Hart, Louise. *The Winning Family: Increasing Self-Esteem in Your Children and Yourself.* Berkeley, CA: Celestial Arts, 1993. Simple, practical advice for parents.

"How Are You Feeling Today?" Poster. Cincinnati, OH: Creative Therapy Associates, 1989. 18" x 24" poster illustrates 30 different feelings, from Exhausted to Ecstatic, Embarrassed to Smug.

Kaufman, Gershen. *Shame: The Power of Caring*. Third edition. Rochester, VT: Schenkman Books, 1992. Clarifies the role shame plays in all aspects of our lives.

Kaufman, Gershen, and Lev Raphael. *Dynamics of Power: Fighting Shame and Building Self-Esteem*. Second edition. Rochester, VT: Schenkman Books, 1991. Teaches essential skills for building self-esteem; shows how psychological health and self-esteem depend on overcoming shame and developing personal power.

Owens, Karen. *Raising Your Child's Inner Self-Esteem: The Authoritative Guide from Infancy Through the Teen Years*. New York: Plenum Publishing, 1995. Explains what to expect from children at each developmental stage; covers topics including shyness, aggression, and children with special needs.

Purkey, William W., and John M. Novak. *Inviting School Success: A Self-Concept Approach to Teaching and Learning*. Third edition. Belmont, CA: Wadsworth Publishing, 1996. Covers teaching skills and techniques that "invite" students into the learning process; demonstrates how the teacher's beliefs and attitudes—including trust, respect, and optimism—enable students to do and be their personal best.

Roehlkepartain, Jolene, and Nancy Leffert. *What Young Children Need to Succeed: Working Together to Build Assets from Birth to Age 11*. Minneapolis, MN: Free Spirit Publishing, 1999. Hundreds of practical, concrete ways to help children start out right and grow up healthy, well-adjusted, and strong.

Zack, Linda R. *Building Self-Esteem Through the Museum of I: 25 Original Projects That Explore and Celebrate the Self*. Minneapolis, MN: Free Spirit Publishing, 1995. Student-centered, student-directed, open-ended projects encourage divergent, original thinking and allow creative expression.

ABOUT THE AUTHORS

Gershen Kaufman was educated at Columbia University and received his Ph.D. in clinical psychology from the University of Rochester. Professor in the Counseling Center and Psychology Department at Michigan State University, he is the author of *Shame: The Power of Caring* (Rochester, VT: Schenkman Books, 1992) and *The Psychology of Shame: Theory and Treatment of Shame-Based Syndromes* (New York: Springer Publishing Co., 1996). He is the coauthor with Lev Raphael of *Dynamics of Power: Fighting Shame and Building Self-Esteem* (Rochester, VT: Schenkman Books, 1991) and *Coming Out of Shame* (New York: Doubleday, 1996).

Lev Raphael was educated at Fordham University and received his M.F.A. in Creative Writing from the University of Massachusetts at Amherst. He holds a Ph.D. in American Studies from Michigan State University, where he has taught as an assistant professor of American Thought and Language. With Gershen Kaufman, he codeveloped and cotaught the program, "Affect and Self-Esteem," on which *Dynamics of Power* and *Stick Up for Yourself!* are based. Book critic for National Public Radio's "The Todd Mundt Show" and "Mysteries" columnist for *The Detroit Free Press*, he is the author of five Nick Hoffman mysteries, most recently *Burning Down the House* (New York: Walker & Co., 2001).

Pamela Espeland has authored and coauthored many books for teens, children, and adults including *Life Lists for Teens, What Kids Need to Succeed, What Teens Need to Succeed, Making the Most of Today, Making Every Day Count,* and *Knowing Me, Knowing You,* all for Free Spirit Publishing.

Other Great Books from Free Spirit

Stick Up for Yourself!
Every Kid's Guide to Personal Power and Positive Self-Esteem
Revised and Updated
by Gershen Kaufman, Ph.D., Lev Raphael, Ph.D., and Pamela Espeland
Realistic, encouraging, how-to advice for kids on being assertive, building relationships, becoming responsible, growing a "feelings vocabulary," making good choices, solving problems, setting goals, and more. For ages 8–12.
$11.95; 128 pp.; softcover; illus.; 6" x 9"

Leader's Guide
For grades 3–7.
$19.95; 128 pp.; softcover; 8½" x 11"

What Young Children Need to Succeed
Working Together to Build Assets from Birth to Age 11
by Jolene L. Roehlkepartain and Nancy Leffert, Ph.D.
Based on groundbreaking research, this book helps adults create a firm foundation for children from day one. You'll find hundreds of practical, concrete ways to build 40 assets in four different age groups. Comprehensive, friendly, and easy-to-use, this book will make anyone an asset builder and a positive influence in children's lives. For parents, teachers, all other caring adults, and children.
$11.95; 320 pp.; softcover; illus.; 5¼" x 8"

Leader's Guide
Ready-to-use workshops for parents, educators, and other adults who work with children in preschool through grade 6.
$19.95; 152 pp.; softcover; 8½" x 11"

True or False? Tests Stink!
by Trevor Romain and Elizabeth Verdick
This book offers proven strategies and practical advice...plus plenty of humor and goofy cartoons. Kids will smile and laugh as they discover tips and information that will help them survive and thrive in all kids of test situations. For ages 8–13.
$9.95; 88 pp.; softcover; illus.; 5⅛" x 7"

Making Every Day Count
Daily Readings for Young People on Solving Problems, Setting Goals, & Feeling Good About Yourself
by Pamela Espeland and Elizabeth Verdick
Each entry in this book of daily readings includes a thought-provoking quotation, a brief essay, and a positive "I"-statement that relates the entry to the reader's own life. For ages 11 & up.
$10.95; 392 pp.; softcover; 4¼" x 6¼"

Making the Most of Today
Daily Readings for Young People on Self-Awareness, Creativity, & Self-Esteem
by Pamela Espeland and Rosemary Wallner
Quotes from figures including Eeyore, Mariah Carey, and Dr. Martin Luther King Jr. guide readers through a year of positive thinking, problem solving, and practical lifeskills—the keys to making the most of every day. For ages 11 & up.
$10.95; 392 pp.; softcover; 4¼" x 6¼"

Too Old for This, Too Young for That!
Your Survival Guide for the Middle-School Years
by Harriet S. Mosatche, Ph.D., and Karen Unger, M.A.
Finally there's a survival guide for the "tweens." Comprehensive, interactive, friendly, and fun, meticulously researched and developmentally appropriate, this book addresses issues that matter to young people this age. Packed with quizzes, anecdotes, stories, surveys, and more, this is just what boys and girls need to make the most of middle school—and beyond. For ages 10–14.
$14.95; 200 pp.; softcover; illus.; 7" x 9"

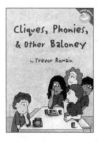

Cliques, Phonies, & Other Baloney
by Trevor Romain
Written for every kid who has ever felt excluded or trapped by a clique, this book blends humor with practical advice as it tackles a serious subject. For ages 8–13.
$9.95; 136 pp.; softcover; illus.; 5⅛" x 7"

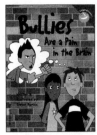
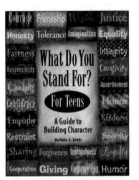

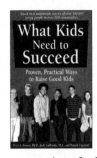

Fast, Friendly, and Easy to Use
www.freespirit.com

Browse the catalog

Info & extras

Many ways to search

Quick check-out

Stop in and see!

Our Web site makes it easy to find the positive, reliable resources you need to empower teens and kids of all ages.

The Catalog.
Start browsing with just one click.

Beyond the Home Page.
Information and extras such as links and downloads.

The Search Box.
Find anything superfast.

Your Voice.
See testimonials from customers like you.

Request the Catalog.
Browse our catalog on paper, too!

The Nitty-Gritty.
Toll-free numbers, online ordering information, and more.

The 411.
News, reviews, awards, and special events.

 Our Web site is a secure commerce site. All of the personal information you enter at our site—including your name, address, and credit card number—is secure. So you can order with confidence when you order online from Free Spirit!

For a fast and easy way to receive our practical tips, helpful information, and special offers, send your email address to upbeatnews@freespirit.com. View a sample letter and our privacy policy at www.freespirit.com.

1.800.735.7323 • fax 612.337.5050 • help4kids@freespirit.com